Freedom Press
12-111 Fourth Ave., Suite 185
St. Catharines, ON L2S 3P5
Printed in the United States of America

ISBN: 978-0-9881691-5-9

Unveiled"
A Canadian Muslim Woman's Struggle against Misogyny, Sharia, and Jihad

Farzana Hassan

FRE3DOM PRESS
CANADA INC.

"The book needs to be read by anyone who has become exasperated by the 'Muslim question', be they Muslim or not. If the book upsets you, then good, Farzana Hassan has done her job and the book has played its part in making one think and question. Imagine, if only a few more Muslims would question, just question, instead of parroting solutions offered in medieval times. Imagine."
• **Tarek Fatah**, author, broadcaster and freedom activist

"The daily chronicle of crimes and horrors committed in the name of Islam makes for depressing reading. Then along comes Farzana Hassan. This new book confirms what some of us already knew: that the author gives a life-line to hope and courage. Brave, resolute, informed, and essential reading."
• **Michael Coren**, author, broadcaster and speaker

"Few debates have gripped us with as much passion and confusion as the one surrounding the rise of Islamist extremism around the world. Farzana Hassan takes on this difficult discussion in her new book, a deeply personal, frank and brave exploration of Islam, Democratic values, Muslims, Islamists and the gaps that divide them."
• **Natasha Fatah**, Toronto-based journalist and documentary producer

"Farzana is one of the most original (and bravest) women writing about religion today."
• **Danielle Crittendon**, blog editor *Huffington Post Canada*

"Farzana Hassan' writings and struggles – to extract Muslims out of the radical interpretations of Islam that lead to demands for Sharia Laws in Western societies, entrenchment of misogyny in the Muslim world, and bloodshed in the name of Islam – are the need of our times."
• **Munir Pervaiz**, Director Progressive Writers Association Canada

Also by Farzana Hassan:

Echoes from the Abyss
Islam, Women, and the Challenges of Today
Prophecy and the Fundamentalist Quest

For
my sons,
staunch advocates of human rights
and my hope for an enlightened generation of Muslim men

Contents

Acknowledgments

Above all, I would like to acknowledge the efforts of countless Muslims like young Malala Yousufzai who have worked fearlessly to oppose the most retrogressive forces within Islam amid great danger and oppression. Such courageous individuals have given me the inspiration to write this book and lend them support in their continuing struggle.

I would also like to acknowledge the efforts of family and friends who have contributed their time to support me in my quest for reform in Muslim societies. In particular, I owe a debt of gratitude to my friend Peter Joyce for providing information on the West's interaction with Muslims.

Writing a book is an onerous task. It demands commitment, time and effort. But this task is made easier when one is surrounded by well-informed people who can shape one's opinions. The influences one imbibes from such interaction are sometimes powerful and compelling. I have met many cultivated and intelligent people during my journey as a reformist Muslim. Feminist authors like Phyllis Chesler, activists like Salma Siddiqui, brave writers like Tarek Fatah, indefatigable crusaders for reform like Munir Pervaiz and revolutionary thinkers like Zuhdi Jasser and Tahir Gora have often offered original and compelling perspectives. To them I offer my profound thanks.

Foreword

The journey Farzana Hassan has embarked upon is a long and lonely expedition in which the certainty of success is as dim as the chance of sunrise on an arctic winter morning. Yet she labours on with a smile that can barely conceal the pain of perseverance. Not only is her path uphill, but it is also strewn with obstacles that alone would make the hardiest of warriors alter course.

Farzana is out to show the Islamic world a mirror that few Muslims wish to see. This book is one they will find difficult to dodge. Her naysayers will try to ridicule her as the epitome of a non-existent self-imagined 'Islamophobia' and dismiss her views of a lightweight who has had no 'training' in Islamic thought.

However, these are the tactics of the Islamist propaganda hate machine whose interests lie in life after death, not the betterment of Muslim hopes and aspirations on this earth of ours. Make no mistake, under her charming smile and friendly demeanour lies the steely foundation of a scholar who knows her religion and the purveyors who employ it to bring death and destruction to this world so as to go to imaginary heavens where pleasures denied on our planet will be aplenty.

I have been on a similar path for the last forty-five years and have had many comrades who have come and gone, abandoned the struggle or intellectualized their abandonment of the fight citing justifiable reasons as they headed for cover, afraid of the not merely physical threats, but just the hint of social ostracizing. But not Farzana, not her.

Our paths met in the mid-2000s in the aftermath of 9/11, as I set out to recruit the dirty dozen who could take on the multi-million dollar Islamist enterprise working as a fifth column, aided by guilt-ridden, bleeding heart white liberals, eager to please the so called victims of "American imperialism" inside America and the West.

All of a sudden the most racist, right-wing misogynist and homophobic elements of western society—Islamists—put on the mask of Dr. King's legacy and were able to convince the liberal-left in US and Canada that they were the true inheritors of the civil rights movement. Few people, let alone Muslims, were able to see through this act of deception carried out in the name of multiculturalism, interfaith pluralism and basic human rights. Farzana Hassan is among the few who could, and this book is one that should open the eyes of

Unveiled:

the folks Lenin referred to as "useful idiots" and I call "sharia-Bolsheviks". In *Unveiled*, Farzana Hassan opens up her life growing up in Pakistan in a family of educated and enlightened Muslims, the product of the golden years of Islam, the late-1800s to the 1950s. *Unveiled* also lifts the curtain on the steep decline of Muslim critical thought since the end of European colonial occupation of India and the Arab world.

In the book, a breezy read, Farzana may not have intended to look back to the future, but just the story of her illustrious family, her parents, siblings, aunts and uncles and the grandmother from England, hearken back to a time which most Muslims born today cannot imagine ever existed in the Islamic world.

The book needs to be read by anyone who has become exasperated by the "Muslim question", be they Muslim or not. If the book upsets you, then good, Farzana Hassan has done her job and the book has played its part in making one think and question. Imagine, if only a few more Muslims would question, just question, instead of parroting solutions offered in medieval times. Imagine.

Tarek Fatah
October 2012

Preface

This book records my experiences as a reform-minded Muslim living in Canada. It analyses and reflects on certain tenets of Islam, Muslim practice and sensibilities. In particular, it records the battles I have fought to oppose fundamentalism in sections of the Canadian Muslim community. I have had to endure some tough campaigns: denouncing terror and violence and speaking out against misogyny in all its insidious forms. During my years as an activist I have had to address a broad range of issues but changing the entrenched ways of diehard Islamists has presented endless pitfalls and scant reward.

My personal struggle has lasted for over a decade. Perhaps 9/11 was the starting point in my public career as a reformist Muslim. That event shook many of us out of our slumber. It impelled us to frame a proper response to the tragedy inflicted by our co-religionists on innocent civilians. Sure, there were already murmurs of disapproval, but more needed to be done; Muslims needed to diagnose and treat the canker that plagues contemporary political Islam.

I therefore pursued an intensive personal study of Islamic precept and practice as an author, writer and activist. I have learned a great deal about the way Islam is practiced, about Muslim attitudes, about geopolitical conflicts and about some of the possible solutions that have almost always eluded the Muslim world. I have also struggled to decipher the many theological and ideological conflicts that emerged during my various discussions on Islam. The conclusions I have drawn spring largely from my ardent desire to help Muslims adjust to a better way of life in Canada.

The Muslim world is undoubtedly in deep turmoil. Young Muslims are confused. Many are struggling to keep their faith in the face of fierce criticism. Some have turned away from it. Others have become more fundamentalist in their religious outlook. I have observed these trends very closely and in order to make sense of them, I have tried to understand the Quran and other Islamic sources at a deeper level.

I approach issues concerning Islam and Muslims sincerely and passionately. However, I must concede at the outset that I am not a scholar of Islam in the orthodox tradition. I have done no formal training in Islamic studies, though I have a working knowledge of the Arabic language, a basic understanding of the Quran and hadith, and considerable knowledge of Islamic history. Most of this I taught myself.

Unveiled:

There seems to be a preponderance of honour killings in Muslim countries. I have tried to examine the reasons for this. Additionally, I have investigated the troubling issue of Muslim rage over criticism of Islam and the prophet Mohammad.

I have encountered opinions on these issues at the grassroots level, where the discussions tend to be the most candid and intimate. Having participated in such debates during my years as a writer and activist on Muslim issues in the West, I have come across the most vigorous discussions on internet forums and in emails. Secondly, plenty of websites host discussions in which some of these opinions are presented in quite a learned way. There is a genuine thirst among both Muslims and non-Muslims to resolve some of these debates. I too have drawn certain conclusions about Islamic belief and practice as a result of these discussions. I elaborate some of these conclusions in the book.

Because my path has been one of introspection, the opinions I have formed from my activism are of course entirely my own. Although I have often conducted research on various issues related to Islamic precept and practice, I cannot claim for sure that I have explored all of the authentic sources on these issues. However, I am reasonably comfortable that my research was sound and my conclusions are backed by the weight of documentation and argument.

Through this small treatise, I hope to make the Western audience understand the Muslim psyche, and I hope to challenge Muslim readers to think candidly about some of the issues I raise in the book.

I feel the Islamic world is at a precipice. This may seem a trite point which may be made at any place and time. Yet Islam is truly at a turning point in its history. We have witnessed the "Arab Spring" in recent years, and at such a crisis point Muslim communities must be steered in the direction of progress rather than decay.

Furthermore, Islam's interaction with the West has increased tremendously. Whether it is due to the West's dependence on Islamic oil, or cultural exchange, or the fact that millions of Muslims have migrated to the West, the gates of interaction can no longer be closed. This relationship between Islam and the West can have profound consequences—for the Islamic world, where social and political change is sorely needed, and for the West, where Islamists wish to introduce institutional change. Only by looking at issues dispassionately can Muslims hope to overcome problems that continue to plague their societies across the world. Only by addressing these can Muslims in the West hope to integrate better into Western society. Muslim civilization is politically, economically, socially and legally backward. Although civil society in many Muslim countries has worked hard to introduce more humane laws and culturally sensitive attitudes, too many inherent problems bedevil the Islamic world. This includes Muslim communities living in Western countries such as Canada.

I am aware that I may offend many among family, friends and co-religionists, but I am convinced I must tackle these debates as openly and plainly as possible. For problems to be solved, an accurate diagnosis is crucial. That is what this book attempts to accomplish, as did my decade-long activism as a reformist Muslim.

I hope that through the pages of this book, young Muslims too will begin to search candidly for answers to contentious questions. I hope that I will also provide a touchstone for many of them who are struggling to keep their faith while attempting to reconcile it with modernity.

Part One
Foundations

Terror Over Blue Skies

It was business as usual in New York. The blue sky glimmered with hope over a bustling city of ten million. But on September 11 2001, that calm and innocence would be lost to a hitherto mysterious enemy, one that would strike—and strike again—with unprecedented ferocity and treachery.

Life was normal that morning in not-too-distant Toronto as well. I had just returned home after dropping my three children off at school. I made a brief stop at the grocery store to pick up some milk for breakfast. As I opened the front door of the house, I heard my husband proclaim in bewilderment: "This is declaring war on America!" He was shaking his head in disbelief.

"What, what, what? What has happened?" I asked nervously. "Why that look?"

But all he could say was "This is declaring war on America. This won't bode well for Muslims in North America."

The television screen in the tiny den of our suburban bungalow in Mississauga flashed the name *al Qaeda* and *bin Laden* as my heart pounded with anxiety and disgust.

"Please God, let these reports be wrong. Please God, let this not be the action of fanatical Muslims," I muttered to myself.

The news broadcaster then said that the terrorist group known as al Qaeda had claimed responsibility for the attacks. The lanky, bearded figure of bin Laden appeared and reappeared on the TV screen. He had made his appearance before as well, but now he seemed everywhere. What a smug, triumphant look, I thought.

Unveiled:

Al Qaeda and Osama bin Laden were at that time only vaguely familiar to me. I recalled that a few years before that tragic day, bin Laden had also attacked the US embassies in Tanzania and Kenya. Like 9/11, these were synchronized attacks, resulting in the deaths of hundreds of innocent people. I recalled that president Clinton had ordered al Qaeda bases bombed in Sudan and Afghanistan. But this time, al Qaeda had struck on US soil.

"This action will spell danger for Muslims!" continued my bewildered husband. "This is war, this is war!" he kept muttering in the background.

The phones began to ring within an hour of the attacks. Our family members in New York were fine. No one had been hurt, my brother's anguished voice told me through the telephone lines. But I could still detect grief. His old friend from school had perished in the attacks.

A niece studying at NYU had also taken the subway toward the twin towers that morning. But all she could express was puzzlement. What was this about? Did any of this have something to do with her as a young Muslim girl studying to improve her professional prospects? How should this affect her plans to complete her studies while her family awaited her return to Lahore, Pakistan?

The luckiest person in our family was my maternal uncle, who was due to board one of the doomed flights from Boston to New York that morning. He narrowly escaped the horrendous death that three thousand other innocent people, including innocent Muslims, faced that day. An emergency at home had kept him from taking the flight.

The TV screen repeated the images of the falling twin towers over the next several days. At home in Toronto, newspapers and television broadcasts continued to cover the 9/11 tragedy, and we Muslims living as a religious minority struggled to keep a brave face amidst questioning looks, censure, guilt, embarrassment and fear.

Pakistan, on the other hand, saw jubilation. Yes, jubilation, even in educated and enlightened circles. Someone had stood up to America, the big bully and "Great Satan". In fact much of the Islamic world expressed joy that America's financial centre had been destroyed, its airline industry hobbled, and the peace of mind of its public shattered and terrorized. Images of jubilant Palestinians dancing in the street appeared on the television screen. They were happy that Israel's biggest supporter had been humiliated by a lone man trudging the hills of Afghanistan, perhaps pondering his own fate after accomplishing his greatest feat ever.

But what did all this mean for the future of Muslims in the West? Was the Muslim world truly at war with the West? Would the West unleash a "crusade"

4

against Islam? President George W. Bush's comments certainly appeared to confirm those fears.

The living rooms and parlours of Muslim homes roared with opinions on many of these concerns. Ours was no different. We also wondered what Islam really stood for. Was terrorism Islamic? Many proclaimed no; such an outrage was a clear deviation from Islamic principles. The Quran was clear that no innocent life was to be taken, that jihad was to be declared only by governments, that Islam is a religion of peace.

Bin Laden, many asserted, had acted on a deviant view. He had launched a jihad against the West based on a vicious misinterpretation—a jihad which he had slyly and cynically been preparing for years. In 1999 he had written a long letter to Americans. He stated his reasons why the attacks would be justified according to Islamic precepts. He said that Islam permitted revenge commensurate with the injury inflicted on Muslims. He accused America of looting the Muslim world by establishing military bases, by digging for oil, by supporting Israel and by killing innocent Palestinians. Bin Laden was defiant and unapologetic about any actions he might take. He would do anything against the West which he had the means to do, and it seemed he had support in countries where Muslims were the majority.

Here in Canada, Muslim activists stepped up their efforts to dispel any negative images of Islam. Islamist organizations like CAIR, ISNA and CIC kept explaining that Islam forbids the killing of civilians. Even George W. Bush agreed. He declared on television that Islam was a peaceful religion and American Muslims loved their country as much as other Americans. Although there was a backlash against Muslims, many North Americans refused to let 9/11 taint their image of Islam.

My mother, stepfather, brother, his wife, and their two sons then lived in Mansfield, Massachusetts. A few days after 9/11 my mother told me that a group of Jewish women had visited the local mosque to express sympathy with the Muslim community, which was beginning to suffer a palpable backlash in that small New England community. The Jewish women had come out strongly to express their solidarity with those who belonged to another religious minority. My mother felt gratitude toward these concerned women. Many of us here in Canada also felt relieved that our fellow Canadians did not hold all Muslims responsible for the attacks. I could sense much sympathy for Muslims in Canada–and some reproach.

Thus began the post-9/11 era for me as a Muslim living in Canada. He is of course now dead, but bin Laden changed the world that day and especially changed the lives of many Muslims like me. My own experience would soon

5

be transformed into one of endless debate with my co-religionists. These debates would involve questions over the essence of Islam. Indeed, 9/11 rocked the world and shook some of us personally as well. Precepts that until now had been left untouched were open for debate and investigation. Truths that had once seemed hewn from stone suddenly appeared sketched in sand. Declarations had turned to questions. Was Islam really a religion of peace? What was the true purpose of jihad in Islam? Did Islam really accord women equal rights? How much in Islam was truth and how much was propaganda or at least interpretation? Was the West out to destroy Islam? Was the Muslim perception of victimization, particularly that perception by Osama bin Laden and his goons, at all justified? Did apostates deserve to be put to the sword? What was the status of non-Muslims in an Islamic country? In the weeks following 9/11, some or all of these questions perplexed Muslims and non-Muslims alike. There was a shifting of loyalties. There was a discarding of ideas. There was also a consolidation of religious identities, sometimes with unimagined and lethal consequences.

The debates were many and seemed to deliver no resolution—nothing at least that would determine clearly what Islam actually stood for. The conundrum began to grow. I found myself in the minority on several issues. The struggle for me after 9/11 was not only between me and the outside world, but between me and my co-religionists, some of them close relatives!

The months and years following 9/11 would see other terrorist attacks. Bali in Indonesia would be bombed, as would Madrid and London. Toronto narrowly escaped an attack with the capture of the infamous Toronto 18. These were Canadian-born men who were conspiring to harm their fellow Canadians. This was radical Islam in action. The loyalties it generated would compel such men to flout all other loyalties. The phenomenon of terrorism seemed unconquerable.

New York car bomber Feisal Shahzad was apprehended by US authorities en route to Dubai in 2006. Once again the world's attention was drawn toward an attempted jihad against innocent Americans. In a lengthy email to his friends in 2006, he asserted that jihad was his "way to fight back when rockets are fired…and Muslim blood flows."[1] In the same email, replete with verses of the Quran, Shahzad claimed that global jihad indeed conformed to the spirit of the holy book. I was perplexed. I wrote to a California blogger by the name of Iftekhar Hai, asking him what he thought of Shahzad's statements. Hai quickly challenged this view. He insisted that the extremist had obviously cherry-picked verses of the Quran in order to pursue his politicized version of Islam.

Hai was clearly a moderate. The supposed need to sort moderate from extremist Muslims was itself troubling to me at that time. The term "moderate Muslim" came into wide circulation after 9/11. Yet the very use of the term seemed a bit discriminatory because it was absent from the vocabularies of other faith communities. There was no need to distinguish moderate Hindus from extremist ones, or moderate Christians or Jews from their extremist counterparts. However, the expression still seemed necessary at the time to separate the majority of Muslims from the tiny violent minority. It was only the murderous activities of the extremist Muslims that had caused so much despair. It was hence necessary to make that distinction in order to spare law-abiding Muslims the stigma and censure.

"Moderate Muslim" Hai had been interviewed in 1998 by Chris Gagne of a think tank called the Stimson Center, where he had said: "Like the United Nations Charter, Islam permits fighting in self-defence, in defence of human rights, or on the part of those who have been expelled forcibly from their homes. It lays down strict rules of combat that include prohibitions against harming civilians, against destroying forest, crops and livestock."[2]

That was a common refrain among moderate Muslims. However, Shahzad, the NY car bomber, would have dismissed the "one excuse that Islam does not allow the killing of innocents."[3] Middle class and educated, he came to embody the modern jihadist profile. Such people led me to investigate the concept of jihad in depth. I have discussed my conclusions on jihad in a subsequent chapter.

But jihad was hardly the only contentious issue troubling me. There was the burning issue of women's treatment in Islam. I had previously read the works of Maryam Jamilah, a convert to Islam from Judaism. She had chosen to live as a co-wife to an assistant to Maulana Maududi, the prominent Pakistani commentator on the Quran. Jamilah argued that the Islamic version of gender equity greatly benefits society. Others, like Fatima Mernissi, had previously argued that Islam clearly discriminated against women. Look at polygamy, wife-beating and the segregation of women, she implored.

Muslim women certainly had to endure brutality in the name of Islam in many countries, including Pakistan, my country of origin. They were being raped but incarcerated for adultery. They were being beaten daily by their husbands and still made to apologize to them. They were being killed in the name of honour when it was they who were defiled. What puzzled me most was that the majority of Muslim women still kept asserting that sharia never discriminated against them.

Were they hamstrung by fear, or did they actually believe this? They implied that culture, independent of religion, was more to blame for the misfortunes of women. Islam in fact defended women's rights. If Ayesha, the prophet Mohammad's young wife chose to hide her famed beauty from strange men by wearing a veil, it was for her own good, they said. "Islam protected rather than marginalized her" was the kind of response I heard from devout Muslim women.

Was Islam a political ideology? Authors Tarek Fatah and Abdullahi An-Naim would soon write books suggesting Islam was primarily a secular faith seeking only a spiritual commitment from its adherents. Soon there were challenges to their assertions. Contemporary Islamists insisted that Islam is political with global ambitions and that it seeks to establish its social, moral, economic, and political system across the globe. One Muslim said in an ongoing internet debate: "We are not leaving the US, we are here to spread Islam all over the US and North America. Thanks to Allah that we already have bought many Christian churches and millions of Christians have already embraced Islam."

Was there such a thing as Islamic pluralism? Moderate Muslims believe that Islam in fact introduced the idea of religious and ethnic pluralism, and that Europeans drew their inspiration to institute pluralism from the enlightenment of Muslim Spain. They have further argued that contemporary Islamic societies would indeed be as pluralistic as Western societies if they remained true to Islamic precepts. On the other hand, the doctrinaire orthodoxy among some Muslims prescribes an Islamic theocracy run under sharia law that would most certainly subjugate women and religious minorities. The Middle East is presently seething with demands for democratic reform. But can the precepts of orthodox Islam ever allow true democracy in Muslim nations?

I encountered these issues in the media and on internet forums almost daily. The non-Muslim world was critical of Islam in the months after 9/11, some say justifiably. But even Muslims like me were debating Islam's values among themselves, some quite candidly and objectively, in order to gain a better understanding of their faith. I now questioned that faith unreservedly, and for that I was labelled an apostate by my co-religionists. The public positions I took were obviously unpopular in Muslim circles. What was I to conclude from my minority status within my community? Were Muslims like Tarek Fatah, Munir Pervaiz Saami, Salma Siddiqui and I some of the only genuine moderates? Or was another category of Muslim to be applied to a tiny group like ours?"Secular Muslim", perhaps? "Reformist Muslim"? Perhaps these terms are simply oxymoronic.

It is assumed that the majority of Muslims espouse moderate views even though they may resent what they consider Western hegemony in Muslim lands. They are moderate in the sense that they reject the killing of innocent people in the name of Islam. The extremists, however, believe these Muslims

8

are "moderate" only because they have not grasped what their faith truly demands of them. I was shocked to read that a Yemeni cleric had issued a fatwa stating it is religiously justified to kill Americans, as they elect governments who kill Muslims. A moderate Muslim called Mubashir Inayat responded to that fatwa by saying that not all Americans elect these governments; therefore, jihad against innocent Americans is not justified. That response was not enough for me. Muslims had to do more; they had to shun the doctrine of militant jihad.

The ideological tussle between the moderates and extremists has been fierce since 9/11. In these fierce debates I have struggled to promote a tolerant strain within Islam, to alleviate the suffering of Muslim women and to protect beleaguered religious minorities in Muslim majority countries. Apart from being branded an apostate, I have been accused of being a sell-out, a Zionist conspirator, a self-hating Muslim, a "whore" for opposing the burka, a shrew who flouts all domestic virtues and a libertine who promotes "immoral secular values".

I have even been insulted by my own relatives. One of them called me a hypocrite, the same label that was hurled at me by a fanatic in March of 2007 who made a threatening call on the answering machine of the Muslim Canadian Congress. He warned author Tarek Fatah and myself that he would slaughter us if we did not stop our "anti-Islam" campaign. Yes, some of my relatives also called me a hypocrite. I told them there were many expressions of Islam, and many different ways of following a Muslim code. They insisted there was only one Islam—and that is the one that had to be restored to its "pristine beauty". They insisted the versions of Islam I spoke of were heresies.

But how could I deny the several different versions of Islam I encountered in the years after 9/11? Which ones were heresies? The plethora of interpretations of Islam had rendered it virtually impossible to claim for sure that such-and-such worldview was the correct one. It had become impossible to define with certainty the essence of Islam. Who were right: the extremists, the moderates, or those who maintained a middle ground?

I set out on a quest for some truthful answers to these questions after 9/11. It is that truth I have been trying hard to unravel in the last decade. It has posed me many personal challenges as a Muslim living in Canada. I have tried to reconcile my Muslim identity with my Canadian identity, for one. I have also encountered roadblocks in trying to bring about reform within my community. But my decade-long activism has shaped my opinions on a diverse set of issues that I discuss in subsequent chapters.

The Sixties Were Peaceful

Things were different from the fanaticism of today when I was growing up in the sixties in Pakistan. Even as a child, I was aware of differences in creed among the people we came in contact with. But there was nothing of the bigotry and fanaticism so evident in today's Pakistan, the second most populous Islamic country in the world.

Our family was educated even in the time of British colonial rule. Some even had degrees from abroad. This was unusual, considering that Indian Muslims were by and large considered irrelevant to the functioning of the country during the Raj. My paternal grandfather had received a law degree from London in the late 1920's. He had also done the unthinkable by bringing back with him a British wife, Winifred Elizabeth.

My paternal grandma came from a large Methodist family. Her strict upbringing had taught her to adjust to any circumstances, but making a move from her native England to a British colony must nonetheless have been a shock to her. The entire neighbourhood had come to visit the *memsahib*. *Mem* was just a contortion of *ma'am*, the honorific given to English women by the indigenous populations. An Englishwoman was revered in those days. An Indian man marrying a *memsahib*? Wow! My paternal grandma continued to be referred to as *memsahib* in the family for as long as I can remember.

My great-grandfather's house on Litton Road, Lahore, was overrun with visitors when Winifred arrived. One of his neighbours was the renowned politician Sir Fazle Hussain, who would later play an active role in the partitioning of India. His eldest daughter would become my elder sister's mother-in-law in 1971.

Unveiled:

Winifred was amused at the attention she received. But she often recalled how kind and welcoming her in-laws had been to her when she arrived in Lahore. They had showered her with valuable gifts: jewellery, saris, and their indispensable assurances that she would have no trouble whatsoever adjusting to a new and strange environment because they would all be there to help and support her.

My eldest aunt was born in 1929. Miriam, or Maryam as she was known in Pakistan, became a well-known journalist. My younger aunt Amina (Lillian) was an accomplished pianist. My father, the youngest of the three in this cross-cultural marriage, is Professor Emeritus of English language and linguistics and currently dean of a university in Islamabad.

I was born into a family of considerable influence. Both my paternal and maternal great-grandfathers were eminent Indians during the time of the Raj, a rather dubious distinction from the perspective of modern sensibilities. However, I am told they were upright men who rose to eminence through the sweat of their brows rather than through betrayal or expediency. Our family indeed had a long tradition of education. One ancestor, who had migrated to the subcontinent from Herat, Afghanistan, was a court physician to the rajah in the northern city of Peshawar.

Apart from being educated, we were also deemed religious elites in a society where religion played a significant role. Being *Syed* meant we were held in respect and awe. And we were Sunni Syeds, not Shia. We were after all the descendents of the prophet Mohammad through his youngest daughter Fatima. Fatima had two sons: Hassan and Hussain. Hassan, the elder, had many wives and hence plenty of progeny. Our family history had recorded us as being his descendents.

Growing up in a privileged environment meant I would be sent to the best missionary school in Lahore. Lahore's well-to-do families always sent their children to Christian schools. Therefore, at that time, two convent schools were considered for my sister and me: Convent of Jesus and Mary, and Sacred Heart. Since my grandfather had sent my mother to Sacred Heart, my older sister and I were enrolled in that school in the sixties. A convent education meant I was fluent in English from the very beginning. That, as well as the fact that I had an English grandmother.

The sixties were peaceful in Pakistan. Or perhaps as a child I was not as acutely aware of the religious and political tensions that simmered under the surface. I recall how we seemed to get along with all of our neighbours. And of course we celebrated Christmas each year because my Protestant grandmother had not converted to Islam. Nor had she ever been expected to convert. She was simply allowed to be who she was. She wore Western dress until the eighties! Perhaps it was the wave of fundamentalism during Ziaul Haqq's time that forced her to change her attire to the more traditional *shalwar kameez*.

I remember singing well-known Christmas carols as my grandmother played the piano. My favourites were *O Come All Ye Faithful* and the *The Virgin Mary Had a Baby Boy*. Ours was one of the rare homes in Lahore that owned a piano in the sixties.

My sister and I did not receive a particularly religious education. Despite the *Syed* label, ours was a secular home; neither was the social climate of the country at that time very religious. No doubt people saw themselves as Muslim in the sense of being different from, say, Christians or Hindus or Sikhs. After all, Pakistan is an ideological state, created on the basis of religious identity. But other than that, there was no particular active religiosity one could discern among Muslims. My family was no different.

The only time such religious fervour surfaced was around Ramadan. People observed Ramadan, the third pillar of Islam, with greater fervour than they observed the five daily prayers, which are the second pillar of Islam. In fact I do not recall any of my aunts and uncles praying regularly. Even my maternal aunts and uncles, some of whom have now turned devoutly religious, did not pray during Ramadan, when it was required that Muslims strive harder for the ultimate blessing of Allah.

I suppose Ramadan was popular because in many ways it was the only festive month. There was the hopeful anticipation of Eid, when family members would get together and share meals and gifts. There were *iftar* parties. Women would have the best clothes stitched for Eid. The latest fashions would be exchanged by young girls in the family. It was a tradition to wear the finest clothes on Eid day. Ramadan in the sixties was more like Christmas. The religious component was there in the background somewhere. But Ramadan and its grand finale in Eid was more about family, dinners, celebrations, the latest fashions, modern jewellery, money, gifts and partying.

Ramadan is austere now. The Wahhabi influence on Muslims has resulted in a less celebratory flavour to Ramadan and Eid. The joy and pageantry of the Ramadan of the sixties has now been replaced with greater emphasis on *salat* (worship), the giving of alms, the performance of voluntary prayers and a more constrained Eid celebration.

Milad un Nabi too was a much celebrated event. This was the Eid of the birthday of the prophet. Pakistan is an odd country of polarities and anomalies. There are those who celebrate the persona of the prophet Mohammad perhaps more than they celebrate the grace of God. These Barelvis believe in observing the birthday of the prophet Mohammad, whereas the Wahhabis shun this version of Eid, sometimes violently. They believe that celebrating the prophet's birthday amounts to deifying him "as the Christians defied Christ." Indeed, there have been violent clashes between Wahhabis and Barelvis in recent years. Any celebratory observance of the faith has come to be regarded as a *biddat* or *biddah* (an innovation that is often seen as an unwarranted accretion to the faith). Celebrating anyone's birthday is considered one such innovation. Anything not done in the time of the prophet is regarded as an inauthentic accretion. In ultra-orthodox Muslim homes, even children's birthdays are never celebrated. Birthday parties in Pakistan were anyhow imported by the British. Indigenous populations did not care much about birthdays. In fact it is not unusual for local Indians or Pakistanis to be unaware of their actual birthdays and therefore ignorant of how old they really are.

Now especially, there is a strong movement among Wahhabis to expunge any or all practices they see as *biddah*. What is or isn't *biddah* is now left to the more fundamentalist custodians of the faith. Wahhabi Islam is increasingly being seen around the Muslim world as the true face of Islam. Therefore anyone espousing that particular strain has the authority conferred on him to interpret the faith.

Despite being brought up in a culturally hybrid and nonreligious environment, I was given to religiosity at an early age. Perhaps it was the influence of my maternal grandfather, whom I adored. He was a warm and kind man who loved children. He was also the only adult in my life who I knew prayed five times a day. No, the daily ritual prayer was not big in the sixties. One day my grandpa (or *ShahJi*, as we all lovingly called him) asked me what I wanted to be when I grew up. I very innocently responded to him by saying I wanted to be a saint. I was his *bazurg bacha* ("saintly child") from then on. And it was he who taught me how to perform the *salat* when I was seven. My paternal grandfather taught me how to recite the *kalima*, the statement of creed that "there is no God but God and Mohammad is the messenger of God."

I was a pious girl. I recall those days in boarding school at Sacred Heart when Ramadan would come around and the Muslim girls would fast secretly. The nuns were not aware that some of us fasted, because we just pretended to eat at meal times. By age ten I had already tried my covert fast in boarding school.

Our missionary school education lacked the intensity of a strictly religious education. I do not recall studying *Islamiyat* until I was in grade six at Sacred Heart. I do remember that the nuns used to insist we pay particular attention to what was being taught in that class. Nice of them to endorse our religion! In fact I do not ever recall the nuns trying to convert us. Other than reciting the Lord's Prayer in the morning, and being inundated with Christianity's symbols such as the cross Mother Jean Francois used to wear, we were free to be the Muslim girls we were.

Religion is as much a lived phenomenon as it is a matter of belief. My maternal grandmother was perpetually unwell. Giving birth to ten children had probably taken a toll on her health. She was not a particularly religious woman but she was one to show reverence to one of the most famous saints of Islam in India, Syed Ali Hajveri. His shrine is situated in the heart of Lahore, where the poor are fed daily. Data Ganjh Bakhsh, as the saint was affectionately called, was known to be charitable and compassionate.

My nani (maternal grandma), or Ammaji, as she was called by all her children and grandchildren, was the eldest daughter of prominent Urdu dramatist Hakim Ahmed Shuja. Ammaji was a woman of considerable talent herself, dishing out poems and short stories as she lay on her bed smoking the hukka. The only time she got up was to go to the bathroom, or to visit the shrine of Data Ganj Bakhsh. That was acceptable at that time. No one questioned such hybrid religiosity then. The religion practiced in the Pakistan of the sixties combined elements of Islamic monotheism and Hindu devotional practices. Whenever Ammaji was faced with a personal challenge, she would visit the shrine, give money to the poor and donate items to adorn the grave of the venerated saint. If she were to engage in such activity now, she would very possibly come under censure even from her own children. The climate has changed drastically since then. In fact, Ali Hajveri's shrine in Lahore was recently the target of vandalism by religious bigots who wished to impose their own fundamentalist brand of Islam on Pakistani Muslims.

Despite being of local Indian stock, my maternal family was on the whole no more religious than my cross-cultural paternal family. My maternal aunts and uncles all went to Oxford and Cambridge for higher education. My mother is a barrister from Lincoln's Inn, London. These were the sixties, and the trend at the time was to go for higher studies to England rather than North America. My youngest maternal uncle even ended up marrying a Western woman.

My mother too was not particularly religious in the sixties. But the seventies brought a double tragedy to my maternal family and my mother turned to God for solace. Her two younger brothers died in 1974. She was particularly close to the thirty-seven-year-old brother who died suddenly of a heart attack. The twenty-eight-year-old died of testicular cancer a month later. Shahji, my maternal grandfather, had already passed away in 1970. Just as well, or he would have been crushed at the passing of his two sons in the prime of their lives. Ammaji was left alone to face this double tragedy. I remember her enduring its memory stoically; she never really talked about it for the rest of her life. She died in 1991.

15

Unveiled:

My parents divorced—another kind of tragedy. They were first cousins, but never got along. My mother remarried. I lovingly called my stepfather *Abujan*, and he and I remained close till his death in 2003. He had been offered a teaching position in the United States. My mother and I were to join him there in 1970 but we first performed the *Umrah*, or smaller pilgrimage, en route to the United States. It was December 1970, a couple of months after Shahji died. We arrived in Jeddah, where a nice Saudi gentleman by the name of Abduallah escorted us around the holy sites.

I have vague recollections of that trip as I was very young at that time. I remember that the precincts of the grand mosque were not as vast as they are now. The mosque at Medina had not yet been rebuilt, but Saudi prosperity was still evident to me. I remember performing the *saee*, the run between the hills of Safa and Marwa where the Matriarch Hagar is supposed to have desperately run in search for water for her infant son Ishmael. Islamic tradition has it that Abraham abandoned the two when Ishmael was only a babe in arms. God had exalted Hagar. It is in commemorating this woman's suffering and resolve that Muslims perform this rite at the *Hajj* and *Umrah*.

I was admitted to Mount Saint Mary's Academy in Fall River, Massachusetts upon arrival in the United States in 1970. Convent education was not in itself a new experience for me; I had of course been educated at a convent school in Lahore as well. But what was new were the short kilts that were part of the uniform at the Academy. That was not something my now devoutly religious mother would permit. She pleaded with Sister Sylvia, the principal at the Academy, to let me wear pants under the uniform. Sister Sylvia simply and magnanimously waived the requirement for me to wear a uniform to school.

This turned out to be more of a misfortune for me at school. I was now the target of bullying, as I came to school every day in a traditional *shalwar kameez*, whereas everyone else was in white top, green plaid skirt and knee socks. Now I was being called "baggy pants" or "Haji Baba". Sister Sylvia realized her mistake but she had given her word to my mother. She instead punished the American girls for not welcoming a visitor and for not accommodating the requirements of my religion. That was the level of tolerance I had experienced from the nuns. Not only was I an oddly dressed student at school, I was also the only Muslim girl attending a Catholic school in that rather parochial and religious southern Massachusetts community.

The girls at "Mount", as our school was called, attended mass every Friday. I was never forced to attend, but I attended it anyway. As I love music, I always enjoyed singing the hymns, however Trinitarian they sounded. That would have been considered a sacrilege on my part, but I didn't really care. I was there mainly for the music and to satisfy my curiosity about another faith.

I also had the very normal pre-teen desire to fit in, so that I would not be ridiculed. I was the school's oddity. While most of my American schoolmates were friendly and warm, some viewed me with tremendous suspicion. Some of the older girls were already dating but I was not allowed to socialize with boys. A nasty rumour soon spread in school that I was a lesbian. This was a hurtful slur when we recall that homosexuality in the early seventies was still much more of a taboo than it is now. Homosexuality is strongly condemned by Islam.

I remember Beverly H. asking me if she wanted to "fix me up with someone". My usual response as a Muslim girl would be "No," which would be followed by bursts of laughter from the girls. I found myself lonely despite being surrounded by very sincere friends like Mary Cassidy, Vivian Laflame, and Patricia Souliere. Mary Cassidy came from a devout Irish Catholic family. The family in time befriended not only me but also the rest of my family. It became routine for us to have Christmas dinner at the house of the Cassidys. Despite both our families coming from markedly different religious traditions, there was at that time never even an attempt to try to convert the other. We simply accepted each other as fellow human beings, and enjoyed each other's company as people of goodwill, despite our profound differences. Mrs Cassidy died of cancer in the early eighties and my mother wept at her funeral.

Indeed, people were friends despite religious differences. Things were pretty settled back then. It was only in the early eighties that I began to detect that wave of Islamism that would germinate with Ziaul Haqq's arrival in Pakistani politics. But that was just Pakistan. This wave would soon engulf the entire Muslim world. It would have ramifications for women and religious minorities most of all. It would appear in laws, in social taboos, in social patterns, in the freedoms of women and in the plight of the downtrodden.

Slowly the environment of the Islamic world would change for the worse. Bigotry would begin to take root and an inflexible orthodoxy would dominate. At that point I was beginning to feel the British and other colonialists did not complete their job. They should have stayed longer to ensure that democratic principles and a culture of tolerance and pluralism were firmly established in the subcontinent. The Islamic world was now riddled with fanaticism of the worst kind: one that would kill and terrorize in the name of religion.

When girls are in their late teens, their parents begin to worry about their marriage prospects. I suppose I was allowed to be something of a rebel when it came to finishing my education before I committed to being bundled off to my husband's home. There had been prospects since I was about seventeen but my mother had said no to them. Usually in Pakistan, even in the higher educated classes, the very first match that comes a girl's way is accepted. I on the other hand married in my mid-twenties after completing my masters in business from the University of Massachusetts.

Dating is a no-no in Pakistan. At least, it was in the late seventies and early eighties, although one would hear of the odd "love marriage". That was a term used to designate a match forged by the couple themselves because of their love for each other, as opposed to an arranged match. People who ended up in a love marriage had had "an affair". In the Western world we apply the term to an adulterous relationship, whereas in the anglicized society of Pakistan, unmarried people were said to have "an affair" when they were merely dating.

It was taboo to have "an affair". Girls who had had them were considered loose. I therefore had to wait for a proposal through proper family channels to be married. The arranged match came from an unlikely source: the principal of my former school, Sacred Heart in Lahore. It was Sister Gonzaga who introduced my husband to our family through one of his older sisters, who taught at the school. My husband had attended Sacred Heart as well.

It turned out my husband's father knew my grandfathers and great-uncle at Lahore's Government College in the 1920s. Our marriage was solemnized at Lahore's Gymkhana Club on the 28th of December 1984. I left Pakistan for Canada soon after my marriage to Shahid.

The religious flavour of Pakistan was changing. I have seen a steady change in social patterns and religious sensibilities since I got married. Pakistan has changed from a somewhat irreligious society in the sixties to a nation heavily infiltrated by Wahhabism—a trend which began after Ziaul Haqq assumed power in 1977. In my youth I had rarely come across women with hijabs. That headdress has primarily been imported into Pakistan from Saudi Arabia. Previously in Pakistan, women who wished to cover their hair simply took one edge of their *duppatas*, the scarf worn around the *shalwar kameez*, and threw it over their heads. Then in the late seventies came the trend in wearing the chadors that were popular in the Khyber Pakhtunwa province of Pakistan. Now there are hijabs galore—and niqabs. This is a sign that the country has moved away from its cultural roots, which happen to be Indian, toward a more Arabized version of Islam, with all its imported symbols, attire and social patterns.

Now sitting-rooms and parlours have turned into mosques. Rarely did I see Pakistanis praying together in the sixties or seventies. Now when it is time to perform one of the five daily prayers at social gatherings, Muslims exhort each other to leave what they are doing and join everyone in prayer, and the pressure to comply with such exhortations is immense. Piety can be a good thing, but enforcing it with such implied coercion cannot be healthy. People should be free to practice their faith as they deem fit. Unfortunately among Muslims there is now a greater emphasis on convergence of belief and ritual. Any narrative that is closer to the Wahhabi point of view wins favour among Muslims these days, which means there is a greater trend towards fundamentalism in religion. Anyone who is seen to challenge this view is considered a heretic and an apostate. That is, to say the least, a very unfortunate situation to be in, as people seen as apostates and heretics can be prime targets for execution. This wave of fundamentalism in Islam has had serious repercussions on the social, political and economic destiny of Islamic nations in recent years.

What Changed My Religious Outlook

In early 2002 my husband and I performed the Hajj, the pilgrimage to Mecca. The men wore two white sheets of cloth when performing the rites of the Hajj. Decorum and tradition demanded simplicity, to remind them that they must all perish one day and that they must never lose sight of the mortality that makes them all equal, regardless of their station in life. They must therefore always display simplicity in their dress, demeanour and lifestyle. The women could perform the rites in their everyday clothes. I felt elated being among so many believers. Surely Islam was being misunderstood across the world, I thought. I searched for answers in the Quran soon after performing the Hajj. Surely I would find something in there that would vindicate Islam.

I felt aggrieved on behalf of Islam and Muslims in those early days after 9/11. Everyone was criticizing Islam. It was just misunderstood, I thought. People just could not grasp the wisdom behind certain Quranic precepts. If there was inequality, it was there for a good reason. God punished for good reason too. The passionate and vigorous discussions on Islamic religious observances continued on internet forums and in email exchanges. There were now websites galore publicizing lay and scholarly opinions on Islamic belief and practice. These opinions seemed contradictory. But I was clearly parroting the orthodox narrative. My perceptions and understanding of my faith would undergo a drastic change in the years that followed.

People often practice their religion in an unthinking manner. For years that is how I observed the various tenets of my faith, without asking the logical questions I may have asked in other aspects of my life. During the decades spanning my own experience as a religious person, I have come across several people inside and outside my family who are otherwise intelligent people, but who prefer to put shutters around their brains when it comes to matters of faith. They will not question some of the most troubling tenets of the religion to which they belong. They would much rather fabricate all sorts of explanations, rationalizations and justifications for anomalies and contradictions that may appear obvious to non-believers or impartial researchers.

Many conservatives also think only religious experts have the right and proper knowledge to interpret faith, and they view the opinions of the laity with suspicion. Yet I firmly believe that anyone who is affected by religious discourse and practice ought to have the right to comment on religious precept. That has been my position ever since I began debating these issues publicly. As a Muslim I have every right to question my faith, to arrive at my own understanding of it, and to practice it according to my very own sensibilities as a unique human being. I am grateful to my adoptive country, Canada, for guaranteeing that right. Canada has taught me the value of free thought and expression. Many from among my very own family and friends have attempted to place restrictions on my entitlement as a free-thinking individual, but I continue to reserve that right and continue to exercise it even as I speak now from the depth of my heart.

I therefore have the right to question the flood of opinions on what Islam mandates, who is right about what, and indeed even who qualifies as a Muslim. On the latter issue, some use "Muslim" as a generic term encompassing all people who believe in a monotheistic God, while the most rigid and doctrinaire would actually exclude many people who call themselves Muslims. For example, Irshad Manji, controversial author of *The Trouble with Islam Today*, has often been labelled an apostate for her views and for the fact that she is a lesbian.

That was also going to be my fate as a reformist Muslim. Those perceptions have not changed in the last ten years. But I struggle almost daily to bring about reform. Perhaps the character of my circle of Muslims has changed a tiny amount as a result; or perhaps it hasn't. Perhaps some Muslims are receptive to my ideas and are just too afraid to acknowledge them; or perhaps they are not. But religion continues to play an important part in our lives as Muslims. We certainly need to calibrate its role as a minority religious community in Canada, in order to ensure a just and equitable society for all.

I had taken a more honest look at my own faith once before in my life. It was in my early twenties. Aspects of its theology, sociology and legal framework already troubled me greatly. I pondered questions like the paradox of evil. I was perplexed that a good God would create evil in the first place. I wondered if evil was a creation of God or a consequence of human action. The latter was one explanation offered by several religious people I met. These were indeed very pressing questions for me, so I also explored the opinions of Muslim theologians, exegetes and philosophers on these issues. There was really very little in what Muslim theologians and philosophers had offered that satisfied my thirst.

Perhaps it was exposure to the Gospel of Barnabas that exasperated me the most. I had thought this Gospel was an accepted Christian text. For Christian readers who might be puzzled by my interest in the Gospels, suffice it to say that Muslims must recognize all Christian and Jewish texts as partially valid. Barnabas is now considered by most to be a medieval forgery. Regardless, its descriptions of hell greatly bothered me. Why would a loving God subject human beings to such endless torment over a simple intellectual error, if it were an error at all? The Gospel of Barnabas turned out to be the piece of literature that would most foment anger in my heart against organized religion. Believe, or else you are doomed eternally! There was little regard for how to live righteously, how to be kind or how to raise good children.

Furthermore, all around me now there was far too much cloning of religious opinion. Everyone in Pakistan had to adhere to the accepted religious narrative or else suffer rebuke from family and possible backlash from the community. Those were the eighties and Ziaul Haqq's Islamic reforms were now embedded in the consciousness of Pakistanis. A segment of the Pakistani public became devoutly religious, while some whole strata of Pakistani society rebelled by criticizing sharia law without the slightest compunction. Others simply recoiled from challenging religious precepts. A common refrain was that this was God's law and even if it seemed unjust, there had to be some wisdom behind it.

Family pressure got me studying Arabic to better understand the Quranic message. A cleric was hired to teach me the basics of Islam and the Quran and impart some basic proficiency in Arabic as a necessary pedagogical tool toward this understanding. My questioning was seen to be leading me astray, and something was needed to prevent estrangement from my faith. Many Muslims question their faith; I was not alone in this questioning. But Islamic scholars have developed an elaborate formula of responses to counteract the doubt that people may have about dogma. The Islamic scholar hired to teach me expounded some of those responses to me. Then came the marriage proposal my mother had been waiting for. A religious man with good family values from a good family background. We were married in 1984, and now I had a new life to look forward to. My eldest son was born three days after our first

23

wedding anniversary. I became an unthinking religious person once again. That state of mind would not change until that catastrophic day in September 2001.

Before 9/11 I had questioned but also accepted the justification offered to explain away inequities. I stopped questioning polygamy. I accepted unequal inheritance shares. I accepted that God had to punish the evildoers.

I thought about these issues even after my marriage but dismissed my own questioning as invalid, based on the rebuttals that already existed as Muslim literature. I now had a new set of family members to impress. My parents-in-law came to live with us the first year of our marriage. My husband had sponsored them to Canada. Religion resumed its role as a force for me. I had become religious once again, but this had more to do with habit than conviction. Actually our convictions as Muslims were never really put to the test. Islam was the absolute truth. We Muslims knew with certainty that the world was oblivious to Islam's beauty and truth.

In 1991 I became pregnant for a third time. My two young sons were now attending school full time. The third child, a much-awaited daughter, had come after a gap. My sons were attending ISNA Canada's Islamic school at that time. The older boy was in grade one while the younger son was in junior kindergarten. Those years at the Islamic school gave me an opportunity to observe an Arab form of Islam that was unknown to me previously. The school is situated off Dixie Road in Mississauga. It now houses the junior branch of the ISNA school, the high school section of which is housed in the large ISNA mosque in Mississauga.

Sending our two sons to the Islamic school was our attempt to give the boys a taste of their heritage and culture. But as I would soon find out, this was not the kind of Islam I had seen practiced in Pakistan, or even in my own family. I came across some of the most devout Muslims in that school community. Many of these men and women had strong and divisive opinions on several burning issues. Political debates flared in and around the classrooms. Even the issue of Israel and Palestine would come up and a certain "sister" narrated the hadith attributed to the prophet of Islam that all the Jews would come together in a place called Israel and then be destroyed by Allah. I did not question this hadith at that time; I was more interested in what my two young sons were learning in English, math and science. Perhaps they would benefit from being exposed to the political conflicts of the world as well.

My sons came home reciting verses of the Quran which they were made to memorize at school. They were also taught Allah's one hundred names. These are known as the *Isma-al-Husna*, or the beautiful names. My younger son took great delight in memorizing and reciting those names. Both boys recited them for the extended family at dinners and their performances were well received.

As both my sons were attending school full-time when I conceived my daughter, I now had time to myself and took the opportunity to study the Quran cover to cover. There were many options at home to undertake this study. We have always had a large library containing Islamic books, commentaries on the Quran and other books of interest. I decided on the well-known documentary of the Quran by Abdullah Yusuf Ali.

On the one hand, there were my children attending a very conservative Islamic school. On the other hand, I was conducting my own study of the Quran. I recall incidents during the time my sons were studying at the school that put me on a collision course with some members of that school community. On one occasion I accompanied my eldest son to a farm on a school trip. The bus was already almost full when the two of us got on. There was just one empty space on the bus and one of my six-year-old son's female classmates was seated on it. I asked my son to sit next to her. Immediately young Noor arose from her seat and stood beside me. I asked her what was wrong. She said she was not allowed to sit next to a boy and that it was *haram*. Anything *haram* in Islam is strictly prohibited. My son and I decided to sit on Noor's seat and she squeezed herself between two other female classmates.

The incident left me rattled. Why were these children being forced to observe gender differences and sexuality issues at such a young age? Who was doing this: was it the school or the parents? Wouldn't exposure to such draconian segregation cause unnecessary paranoia in the minds of these very young children? I began to wonder if exposing my children to such attitudes was the right thing to do.

I also recall that incident when someone poked me from behind during prayer and told me a strand of my hair was exposed. Not wanting to take issue, I simply complied but noted with dismay how much triviality fundamentalist Muslims had become preoccupied with. Why would God be concerned if a little bit of my hair was exposed during prayer? Another incident happened outside my younger son's JK class. The night before, we had taken our two boys out to Burger King. Typical of children, they were happy to receive the Burger King crowns. My younger son decided to wear his hat to school the next morning. I was rudely questioned by one of the other parents about why I ate at Burger King. "Sister, don't you now how these kafirs make the burgers? Why do you eat non-halal meat?" I told her we only ate the fish burgers. I told her these were just kids having a bit of innocent fun. She shook her head and told me I was making a very big mistake by being so cavalier about Islamic precept. I

25

stayed quiet and went about my business, reading the Quran and drawing my own conclusions from Abdullah Yusuf Ali's commentary.

What struck me most about my study of the Quran was its simple and direct theology. Page after page spoke of the oneness of God. The Quran's emphasis is on purity of doctrine and belief. How different it was from Christianity and its triune God, I thought. I saw unity around me as well. I concluded that this was the right understanding of why we are here, what purpose we serve by being here and why it was necessary to worship God. Allah simply meant the deity, and the deity belonged to everyone. Islam was a natural and universal religion and well suited to human nature. I came closer to God and suppressed my own questioning of many of Islam's social regulations that even then festered below the surface. God in his infinite wisdom must have known what to prescribe for human beings. Indeed, I was parroting much of what other devoutly religious people were asserting.

My daughter was born in June 1992, when my sons were still attending the ISNA Islamic school in Mississauga. My husband worked swiftly to reserve a spot in the school for our daughter. Our family made a temporary move to Lahore that year, as my husband wanted to explore business opportunities there. The religious education of my children continued in Pakistan. Like other Pakistani families, we hired a local cleric to teach the boys how to read the Quran in Arabic. Most people in Pakistan can read Arabic script without fully understanding the meanings. The two boys soon finished reading the Quran. They would also go for Friday prayers to the mosque with their father.

Despite my doubts, I had retained an innate religiosity. It compelled me to pray five times a day, something I have done since I was fifteen years old. But I was not particularly interested in continuing my studies of the Quran at that time as my infant daughter needed my full attention.

My husband's business ventures did not bear fruit in a country where every tier of every public department is riddled with corruption. We decided to move back to Canada in 1995. My daughter was three and still enrolled at the ISNA Islamic school. Upon return to Canada, we received a phone call from the school that in September of the following year she would be ready to join junior kindergarten. I had to make a decision. This was my daughter. Would I subject her to the discrimination Muslim girls face in Islamic schools? By now I was convinced that something was not right with the way girls were being treated at the school. For one, they always prayed behind the boys. The administration and staff at the school had retrogressive views, it seemed to me. No. Not even my sons would attend the school now, even though they still had their spots reserved there.

We decided instead to enrol the children at the neighbourhood public school that year. That proved to be a good decision in many ways. In particular, I noticed from the outset the tolerance of diversity that the public school environment offered. The staff consistently treated children of all races and beliefs equally. No teacher proclaimed who was going to heaven or hell. There were Eid celebrations, just as there were celebrations for Diwali, Christmas and Hanukkah. My daughter also went to the neighbourhood nursery school, where she forged lasting friendships with children from diverse backgrounds.

This was all new to me, and a welcome change from what I had observed in the ISNA school. Here diversity was prized; at ISNA it was shunned. Because of the welcoming atmosphere, I became a very active member of that school community, volunteering hours and joining the parent council. At the public school, my children were also exposed to various art forms—and of course music, something that was very close to my heart. My elder son, as well as my daughter, would later discover an extraordinary talent for music.

Discipline was also different. The children were chided gently, rather than having their ears twisted over minor religious infractions—a common occurrence at the Islamic school. Old-style discipline was still in vogue at the Islamic school in the early nineties. I am not sure if that is still the case. The teachers at the public school used progressive and enlightened teaching methods. My elder son graduated from the public school and my younger two were soon identified as "gifted" by the school and transferred to Thorn Lodge Public School in Mississauga. There they had an even better chance of learning music, drama and arts.

The 9/11 tragedy occurred when my daughter had just joined Thorn Lodge and my younger son was in grade nine at Woodlands secondary school. What he told me one morning caused me considerable anxiety. Muslims across North America experienced some backlash in the months following 9/11. My fourteen-year-old son experienced it first-hand from the bus driver who took him to school each morning. For days after 9/11, she ranted about how evil Muslims were, how much they should be despised and how they should all be taken to an island and killed. Whether her antagonism stemmed from white supremacist hatred or simply anger toward Muslims was unclear, but each morning my son understandably felt uncomfortable because of it. I am not sure if she even knew that my son was Muslim. Perhaps she said all this not realizing that some of the passengers may indeed have been of the Muslim faith. I was concerned not only for my son's safety but also for his emotional wellbeing.

I knew at that time that many Muslim women had decided to remove their hijabs in order not to be associated with the terrorists, as there had been unconfirmed reports of Muslim women being attacked by angry Americans. I decided to report the bus driver to the school principal. She immediately took action: she contacted the bus company and the driver was duly disciplined. My son never heard a peep from her about Muslims being evil after that incident. But the actions of the bus company and the willingness of the school to address my concern proved to me how much tolerance for diversity there was in this country. The 9/11 catastrophe had generated a great deal of anger toward Muslims, but it had also generated immense sympathy. Even George W. Bush went out of his way to ensure that 9/11 would not define all Muslims. He took measures to prevent their religion from being demonized.

Indeed, the backlash against Muslims angered me somewhat. Surely we were not all bad. I certainly did not condone the attacks on the World Trade Center and the Pentagon. But an aunt of mine through marriage was apparently elated. She said that what happened that day was the best thing that could happen because America was getting some of its own back. I was appalled

at such callousness. Those dreadful images of innocent people jumping from the ninetieth floor were etched on my brain.

At that time it seemed to me that the whole world was against Islam. I remember listening to a broadcast on CFRB and responding to it with a great deal of anger for vilifying Islam and Muslims. Until that time I had just been a full-time mother. The 9/11 attacks threw me out into the world. I had to do something to dispel the image that Muslims were all terrorists. Yes, Islam was being practiced in a very negative way by some adherents. I too had found orthodox Islamic practice distasteful. That was why I had refused to let my children be subjected to a very conservative and fundamentalist brand of Islam at the ISNA school. My own understanding of Islam was very different from the way it was practiced there. It would turn out that my understanding of Islam would undergo another change, after I stepped into public life and became involved in public theological debates.

I started writing for the Mississauga News as a guest columnist soon after 9/11. What I expressed at that time was a visceral reaction to the negativity about Islam that I saw around me, rather than a well-considered response. Some Muslims have not been able to overcome that visceral reaction, which accounts for their continued hostility toward the West. I said that the West needed to understand that Muslims felt ravaged by Western policy in Israel, Kashmir, Chechnya and generally in the Middle East. But even at that point I knew terrorism had to be condemned. That is when I joined Muslims Against Terrorism as president of the Mississauga chapter. This was a potent way of telling the world we were not all terrorists. I would eventually leave that organization to join the Muslim Canadian Congress.

I was now in public life and engaging in open debate about several issues pertaining to Islam. I entered these public debates as any other Muslim may have done. Muslims are taught never to question their faith. They are never to doubt the accepted narrative. They are to respect and revere the prophet more than their own kin. Even if there are social inequalities in the fabric of Islam, they are to be seen as derived from divine commandments and never questioned. God in his infinite wisdom must have had a reason to ordain these inequalities. His social and legal commandments must, in some unseen way, bring harmony to all of humanity.

Muslims who dare to question are provided with an elaborate rationale to justify these inequalities. Women have a less rapacious sexual urge, and therefore no entitlement to contract multiple marriages. They do not have the responsibility to provide for their families, therefore they are entitled to only half of any inheritance. They must listen to everything their husbands tell them, so that family unity is not compromised. Minorities in Muslim lands must pay the *jizya* (tax) because they are not required to go on jihad, and so forth. Hence there exists a preset formula of responses for everything, setting the Muslim mind in stone. Rarely are Muslims able to break loose from this internal logic that seems to permeate all their religious experience.

I entered public debates with the very same mindset. Any objections to Islam stemmed from an ignorance about it. Non-Muslims simply did not understand that Islam was a very modern and progressive faith. With that outlook I organized a series of lectures entitled Islam 101, a course designed by Syed Soharwardy, then president of the National body of Muslims Against Terrorism and the Islamic Supreme Council of Canada. The lectures were delivered at a local branch of the Mississauga library system. I invited speakers mostly from the traditional school of thought, including members of the ISNA community, to explain to non-Muslims the reasons for certain Islamic social regulations.

The talks included content about Islam's social, economic, political and theological systems. I organized these lectures until 2003, when the debate on sharia broke out in Ontario. I had naturally been exposed to orthodox Islam's rationale and by this point I had begun to find it inadequate in explaining away the inequalities. A local writer, who has written several articles on Islam and women, was one of the speakers at two of these events. She stated plainly that Islam does not treat men and women equally, because men have an edge over women and that unequal treatment is therefore quite reasonable. Ask other Muslim women and they would likely come up with a similar response.

After being so thoroughly exposed to the orthodoxy's rationale, I began to feel uneasy about many sharia stipulations. That was one of the reasons I began to oppose sharia in Ontario in 2003. Several reports of beheadings of gay people in Iran and stoning of women in parts of the Islamic world further heightened my unease about sharia's strictures. In Nigeria it was Amina Lawal, in Somalia it was Aisha Ibrahim Duhulow, in Iraq it was Dua Khalil. Almost invariably the victims were women. Was there something in sharia that left women more vulnerable to such retribution? For example, why were the men with whom these women had allegedly committed adultery not being held to account? The answers to me were simple: the laws were indeed flawed. I was now beginning to step out of the box, to shun orthodox Islam's internal logic and examine its various tenets and practices in a more objective manner.

Our family went to Saudi Arabia in 2005 to perform the *Umrah*, or the smaller pilgrimage. My daughter and I were of course covered in hijabs and abayas. On one occasion, my daughter was scolded by another worshiper because her hair was exposed during prayer. My daughter remarked that she found Saudi women unfriendly. Upon our return to Canada, she began asking all sorts of questions about Islam. She once asked me how I knew Islam was the one true religion. Didn't the faithful from other faith traditions also believe their religion was the absolute truth? She noticed there were no non-Muslims in Mecca and Medina. Why were non-Muslims treated in this manner?

As my own grandmother was Methodist, the plight of Christian, Hindu, Sikh and other religious minorities in Muslim lands always caused me some concern. After 9/11 there was a series of church burnings in Pakistan. The rabid fundamentalists were busy terrorizing any innocent people who belonged to a different faith community from them. Even the less rabid Muslims were targets of violence. In January of 2011, Salman Taseer, the governor of Punjab, was shot dead for opposing Pakistan's blasphemy laws in defence of a Christian woman, Asia Bibi.

I was there when the assassination took place. In fact, I had just ten minutes earlier visited the market where the governor was shot dead. There was jubilation on the streets of Islamabad. That was the level of bigotry I witnessed first hand over a heinous murder. There was something profoundly pathological about such practices. Many proclaimed that true Islam demanded severe action against a blasphemer like Taseer. Two months later Shahbaz Bhatti, the Christian minister of minority affairs, was also assassinated over the same issue. As for Asia Bibi, she still languishes in prison awaiting execution at any time: an event which the mullahs and clerics are excitedly awaiting.

It is tragic that religious sensibilities in the Islamic world have changed for the worse. This change has estranged some of us from the faith tradition with which we grew up. I am still a committed Muslim, but I cannot endorse orthodox Islam's institutions, its prescriptions for women, its punitive systems, its discriminatory sharia provisions or its treatment of minorities.

Many would think that I have strayed outside the fold of Islam. However, I believe I retain the right to call myself a Muslim for several reasons. The Quran itself states that anyone who continues calling herself Muslim must be acknowledged as such. Furthermore, I uphold the unity of God, which is Islam's central doctrine. I am also an observant Muslim, who prays and gives alms to the poor. Additionally, I subscribe to Islam's ethics, in that I do not lie, steal or cheat.

What I do not subscribe to is sharia law as interpreted by the classical jurists. I also believe in a fresh approach to the Quran, and believe in wholly discarding hadith literature that contains suspect, contradictory and misogynistic information. There are also several hadith that depict the prophet in extremely negative light. We may protest so-called anti-Islam movies but we cannot deny the fact that the sources of these movies are in our own Islamic literature. Perhaps because of these ongoing controversies, I have lost the conviction of a devout believer.

I state this with a degree of sadness, as I have also lost the solace I used to derive from my faith—the kind of solace people of faith derive in times of personal crisis or adversity. I have also developed my own sense of morality that is significantly different from that of the orthodoxy's. Perhaps Islam can be modernized and moderated. But until that happens, I will continue to question and challenge orthodox interpretations and understandings of Islam.

Tales of Honour-Based Violence

The Soviets were driven out of Afghanistan in 1989. There had been a massive influx of Afghan refugees into Pakistan during the prolonged war, especially into the northern areas of the country. Afghans had rightly felt that the Soviets had depleted their country of its wealth and resources. Soon the warlords gained control. The country was stripped of its leaders, with the best brains taking themselves into exile. By the time civil war erupted in Afghanistan, many affluent Afghans had also decided that the conditions there were too dangerous, especially for the women in the family. Such was the lot of one family I came to know during my short annual visits to Pakistan. These were Afghan refugees who had made Pakistan their temporary abode before migrating to Canada.

I happened to meet the family through mutual friends. The young daughter told me the circumstances of their escape into Pakistan. She said her memories of that escape remained fresh. How could she ever forget the deafening roar of gunshots as they drove through the craggy terrain of the Khyber Pass? Although they had traveled in an enclosed military jeep across to the security of Pakistan, courtesy of friends and Pakhtun relations, none of them had felt safe. But "Baba", the dad, said they had to escape, not only from the havoc of war, but also from the developing religious fanaticism. It was as if God had unleashed His wrath on a quarrelsome people. When people were denied the right to dream, to be themselves, they had no choice but to flee from the tyranny.

With much despair but sure conviction, Baba had left his once thriving practice as a physician to resettle in Murree, a hill resort in the northern region of

Unveiled:

Punjab, Pakistan. Amma, his forty-six-year-old wife, was reluctant to abandon her beloved house in Kabul, but things had become too dangerous: women were beaten for wearing makeup; girls were barred from attending school; women were raped and accused of adultery.

Unsettling as the change was, both husband and wife knew that in the long run this was the best thing to do. They arrived in Murree safely, Baba, Amma, seventeen-year-old Zameer, and fifteen-year-old Gulmeena.

Although foreign born, their family came to epitomize the values of their adoptive country once they arrived there. Now the quintessential upper middle class Pakistani family, they were practicing a hybrid sort of Islam, adhering outwardly to its rituals while shunning anything that might conflict with comfortable Western values and culture. Such indeed was the legacy of the British Raj. The colonists had left a permanent imprint on the inhabitants of the Near East and South Asia. To be considered "civilized", one had to adopt the traditions, values and at times even the attire and mannerisms of the ruling English. Learning how to speak their language was considered genteel. English medium schools were the certain choice for anyone who could afford them, hence Murree's famous Convent of Jesus and Mary for Gulmeena. My family owns a summer home at the foot of the hill where this missionary school is located, and that is how I came to know Gulmeena.

They quickly adjusted to life in Murree, but Amma and Baba had to endure the pain of relocating in a foreign land. After all, they were faced with a new set of people to impress, foreign rules to obey, and new customs and routines to adopt, and all this took a heavy toll on them. Gulmeena said that her parents didn't get along very well during their first few months in Pakistan.

She and Zameer themselves had to tackle some challenges as youngsters growing up in Pakistan. Zameer had become friendly with a young domestic worker by the name of Tehmina who lured him into a not-so-innocent romance. With her rustic northern charm, rosy cheeks and hazel eyes, this beautiful twenty-year-old Pakhtun woman was quite the temptress. She had often caught Baba eyeing her as well, but Zameer was the one utterly dazzled by her charms.

Gulmeena was to stay quiet when she caught them kissing at midnight just outside the door of the kitchen. Any hullabaloo over this incident would have likely cost Tehmina her life in a country where the honour of women is the most prized yet most dispensable possession. Women who value their lives dare not disgrace their male relatives by committing acts of indiscretion. Tehmina and her kind were treading a dangerous path in those remote and parochial towns of northern Pakistan. Honour killings are the prevailing form of justice in a land where adultery and fornication are criminalized but rape

34

goes unpunished, thanks to the country's sharia law requiring a girl or woman who claimed she had been molested or raped to produce witnesses to attest her statement.

Tribal or family honour is restored by savage retribution. If their fathers, brothers, uncles, grandfathers, sons or nephews do not take appropriate measures to punish the offence, they are seen as cowards with no moral sense. They could never again hold their heads up in society.

Tehmina knew this all too well. Her young cousin Zuriya and her boyfriend had only recently been hacked to death by the girl's family. Those young lovers had been caught kissing behind a tree by the girl's younger brother, who promptly reported the incident to his father because his sister had hurt his pride. Soon the scandal became the talk of the entire village and neighbouring community and the teenage lovers had to be put to death.

It was slightly different for girls from high society. They would not be subject to this type of tribal justice in the same manner Tehmina would, but they would still be rebuked and blacklisted as "flirts". An underlying fear of not finding a suitable match at the desired social level probably accounted for the stigma.

Gulmeena told me that although her father had escaped Afghanistan to avoid the Taliban, his own moralizing on Islamic issues reached a new peak. He had begun to study Islam systematically the summer they arrived in Pakistan, perhaps because he was looking for a sense of identity in a new setting. Inwardly, he felt much closer to his faith than he had ever felt before. He read several popular translations of the Quran and began a comparative study of its text.

Gulmeena told me that Baba quoted the Quran fluently and frequently. What disturbed her most was his frequent reference to the virtues of polygamy and why the Quran sanctioned it.

"The Quran gives us tremendous insight into human nature," he told her once. "You see, it is the Creator who is himself the author. Why wouldn't He know what is good for his creation? He knows that men are by nature polygamous. Men can love many women at the same time but a woman can only love one man."

Women in Pakistan are placed on a pedestal, sometimes to their own detriment. They are treated as madonnas who can do no wrong. They are held to a higher standard and if they fall short of it, they are punished more severely. Men, on the other hand, are deemed depraved. Since they are "polygamous by nature", they can marry a second, third and fourth time and philander all they want. That is their nature, but women–no, they must never transgress, as they are goddesses, not humans! If they do, they may be killed.

Unveiled:

Gulmeena had drawn my attention to these issues after relating her stories during that summer in Murree. I was now afraid for Tehmina. She would have to be very careful indeed. Here was Gulmeena narrating the peccadilloes of people she knew. I remembered that when I was about seventeen years old, our family had provided refuge to a former domestic helper who had married for love. His wife came from the southern Punjabi city of Multan. When she met Mai'ma, our former employee, at a village wedding, she was already betrothed to her cousin. But they met and fell in love. Their families of course were opposed to the match as Mussarat was already engaged. Breaking the engagement would have brought them dishonour.

She was a good-looking woman: tall, willowy, and olive-skinned. He doted on her. They had run away from Multan to avoid the families' wrath and for a while lived in our servants' quarters. I also remember that they left suddenly for another location as they feared their families had obtained knowledge of their whereabouts. They had justifiably feared reprisals. Honour killings would have been a real possibility in this case; the couple could have been hunted down and killed. This was all to preserve family honour, and no law could protect them.

I kept abreast of the issue of honour killings in Pakistan after my encounters with Gulmeena in the early nineties. It was only recently that honour killings would be declared a crime in Pakistan. On another visit to Pakistan I learnt about the Saima Sarwar case, and that Asma Jahangir, a well- known human rights activist and lawyer in Pakistan, was involved. The murder actually took place in the office of Asma Jahangir, who was the deceased girl's lawyer.

Saima Sarwar was a twenty-nine-year-old mother of two who was killed by gunmen hired by her family. Saima had been in a loveless marriage and sought divorce from her husband. She had been estranged from him for four years before the murder and had lived with her own parents during that time. Her husband continued to live in their marital home in Peshawar.

Divorce, too, carries a stigma for women in Pakistan. The parents bitterly opposed Saima's divorce, because it would have meant dishonour for their family. But Saima was adamant, and she fled to Lahore seeking shelter at a local women's NGO called "Dastak". There she approached the two well-known lawyers, Asma Jahangir and her sister Hina Jilani. I remembered Asma from a rally we participated in against the half *diyat* (blood money) issue back in 1982.

The family seemed to relent and agree that a divorce would be acceptable after it became clear to them that Saima would not return to her husband under any circumstances. Saima agreed to meet only her mother to hand over the divorce papers. This meeting would take place in Hina Jilani's office. The mother, however, did not come alone. She came with the killer, who fired a single shot at Saima, killing her instantly. He also fired at Hina Jilani but missed. Jilani's security guard then shot and killed the gunman.

This case shook all of civil society in Pakistan. It was tragic at several levels. Even her own family could not support the need of this young mother to escape from an abusive marriage. Perhaps the most heartrending aspect of this case was that her own family was responsible for this girl's murder. The girl's own mother was an accomplice. It invokes memories of the Shafia case right here in Canada, in which Mrs Shafia recently conspired to kill her own three daughters and their step-mother.

Saima had been married off to her cousin, a wealthy businessman, in Peshawar. It was widely known that Saima's family had connections with the police department and secretariat, and when a family has such connections it is possible literally to get away with murder.

That was Pakistan, but we have seen the lethal effects of this violent misogyny within Canada's own borders. Aqsa Pervez was a sixteen-year-old student at Applewood Heights school in Mississauga. She was a normal, healthy teenager with normal, healthy interests. She simply wanted to fit in. She wanted to wear nice clothes, she had a natural interest in boys and she was well adjusted in school.

Yet at home things were oppressive for Aqsa. Her father and older brother had turned religious, to the extent that Islam became paramount in their lives. They wished to impose their brand of Islam on young Aqsa, but she rebelled. She refused to wear the hijab or to give up her interest in boys. On the fateful day, her brother Waqas lured her home and strangled her. I heard the news at seven in the morning that a young girl was fighting for her life, and later that she had succumbed to her injuries.

Aqsa had moved in with one of her friends before the murder. She had been afraid for some time that she might fall victim to such a fate. She had been threatened with beatings if she refused to comply with restrictions. She was not wrong. Her father phoned police that morning to let them know about the attack. When the medics attended, Aqsa was still alive but was rushed to hospital with life-threatening injuries. She was later rushed to the Hospital for Sick Children, where she died. Both father and son were sentenced to life in prison. But this tragic death sparked many debates about honour killings: why they happen, why they are so prevalent in Islamic societies and whether the phenomenon is primarily cultural or has religious undertones.

Unveiled:

I later handled many interviews about the mindset that produces killers who murder their own daughters in the name of family honour. This was the worst expression of parental authority. This was also religiosity at its most destructive. During the media circuits, I had mentioned that the killing in Aqsa's case was done for religious reasons: her family's demand that she wear the hijab, that she shun her Western lifestyle and that she stop being an embarrassment to the family. The issues over which she was killed were clearly religious.

But did Islam really ask people to kill their daughters in the name of honour? In pre-Islamic Arabia it was customary for Arab men to bury their daughters alive. This practice was driven by the fear that some day these girls might bring dishonour to the family. Islam actually put an end to that practice. But something about that desert culture generated paranoia about female sexuality. It was women who could get pregnant, and this meant that their conduct would have to be strictly monitored. This also had a lot to do with how society viewed men in authority. Control had to be exercised over the flocks–animal and human–for which a man was responsible. Tribal prestige was tied in with concepts of masculinity, power and dominance. Independence shown by any women only served to show that the man controlling them was weak. His only option would be to take the lives of these women or to punish them severely to retrieve lost honour.

After Aqsa's tragic death, many Muslim organizations here in Canada insisted that honour killings were a cultural phenomenon, and that they had absolutely nothing to do with Islam. I would once again embark on a study of the Quran to see if their statements had any merit, or if they were missing the point somewhere. After all, honour killings seemed very prevalent in Islamic countries.

At that time, I was also dismayed at the reaction of many in the Muslim community. Some in the conservative circles said Aqsa merely got what she deserved, as she had disobeyed her father. She may have even been pregnant, some concluded. I was shocked at this callousness over the death of a young person who simply wished to lead her life as a normal Canadian. I had hoped that the local Islamic leaders would clearly condemn Aqsa's killing. Encouragingly, some imams said that children should be chided gently, but many Muslims simply shrugged off this tragedy as a domestic dispute gone awry. This was the natural outcome of a child's rebellion. The girl should have listened, they said.

Then came the Shafia honour killings—a gruesome saga of a family destroyed by medieval notions of honour and a strict adherence to the Islamic faith. This was a family of contradictions. The father was himself in a polygamous marriage. His ex-wife, Rona Amir Mohammad, stepmother to the three slain teenage Shafia girls, was simply biding her time as she wanted to opt out of her loveless marriage with Mr Shafia. She was treated more like a maid in the marriage arrangement. The older girl had been forced to annul her marriage to her friend. The father had asked the son to keep an eye on the girls. And they were called sluts by their own father for dressing provocatively.

The younger two girls were following in the footsteps of the older sister. The Shafia father had often indicated that these girls deserved to die because they were dishonouring Islam by their behaviour. He had expressed his anger to family and friends. On June 30 2009 a car was found submerged in the docks in Kingston. In it were Rona Amir Mohammad and her three stepdaughters: Zainab, Sahar and Geeti, the thirteen-year-old. Police immediately detected something suspicious; this was no ordinary accident. Sure enough, the father, son and mother were arrested and the gruesome details of the murders began to emerge.

It is interesting to consider what connected the killings of Aqsa Pevez and the Shafia girls, and to wonder what both had to do with the kinds of expectations Islamic culture placed on them as women. The families originated from two different cultures–Pakistan and Afghanistan–but shared the same faith.

The murder of Jassi Sidhu also attained a very high profile. But Jassi Sidhu was a Sikh girl. She worked in a salon. Jassi was in love with a man, Sukhwinder, whom her family considered too lowly for her, but the two married and fled to India. They were soon hunted down and the poor woman was abducted and killed, upon orders of the uncle and mother, though these charges are unproven as yet. After the act, the murderers allegedly contacted the uncle and mother. Sukhwinder, who had been beaten and left to die, miraculously survived. However, he was accused of rape, a charge levelled by one of Jassi's relatives. He served a four year prison term as a result.

Crimes like these often go unnoticed even in Western countries where there is redress and better law enforcement. Recently, the gruesome details emerged of a heinous honour killing of a seventeen-year-old British girl by the name of Shafelia Ahmed. This very bright student had dreams of becoming a lawyer. She was known to be an A-level student in school. Her dream came to a brutal end at the hands of her own parents in 2004. Her decomposed body was found in the Lake District of England soon after the crime and simply labelled a "vile murder". In fact, that murder took place at home and at the behest of her own mother, who had asked the father simply to "finish the job". It was only in late 2011 that the parents were apprehended once again and charged with their daughter's murder.

The younger sister finally revealed details of the incident after reaching adult-hood. As a child she was threatened not to say anything or else she would meet the same fate as her unfortunate older sister. Shafelia was being forced into an arranged marriage. This is common even among the educated, elite classes in Pakistan. Children must marry according to their parents' wishes or else their family pride and honour could be compromised. Issues of status and dynamics between relations come into play in such arrangements.

The parents had not reported the girl missing, as she had tried to run away from home in 2003 to escape the prospect of the arranged marriage. The police arrested the parents in 2003 but released them in 2004 after there was insufficient evidence to charge them. Thankfully they have been convicted now.

I discuss the phenomenon of honour killings in the next chapter in some detail.

Part Two
Discussions

Honour Killings: Causes and Solutions

Honour killings are on the rise in Pakistan. According to the latest reports, a thousand women are killed in Pakistan each year, and similar honour killings take place in other parts of the Islamic world. To be fair, honour killings also occur in parts of the world that are not Islamic but continue to be extremely patriarchal. One troubling aspect of these statistics is also under-reporting, as most honour killings are covert operations.

The idea of honour is rooted in the medieval notion that men own women, and that men are therefore responsible for the conduct of "their" women. The supervision of women in patriarchal societies of the Middle East produces callousness, cold-hearted oppression, massive abuse of parental authority and even savagery. I have written about honour killings in various newspapers and journals on a number of occasions. As summarized below from my own writings, the causes of honour killings are plenty but all break any code of morality or decency.

A common perception is that women are the only victims of honour crimes. However, men have also faced such retribution, usually on accusations of adultery, homosexuality or fornication. Of course, women are held responsible if they can be. The Shafia trial in Ontario revealed that women can also be accomplices in the crime. Mothers have threatened their daughters with reprisals if they are seen with boys or if they are suspected of having friendships with boys. But while it is true that not all victims of honour killings are women and not all perpetrators of these crimes are men, the issue is nonetheless greatly divided along gender lines according to who is the most vulnerable.

43

Unveiled:

Some statistics need to be considered here. According to the Human Rights Commission of Pakistan, in 2011 alone 675 women and girls were murdered by their family members for allegedly bringing dishonour to their families. Also according to the report of the commission, seventy-one of the victims were children under eighteen. The women were either accused of having illicit relations with men, sometimes based on mere suspicion, or they had refused a match proposed by the family. Sometimes women were killed in the name of honour simply because they were raped. In other words they had become victims twice. Other actions that could be perceived as bringing dishonour included the following: dressing provocatively, seeking divorce from an abusive spouse, or simply being suspected of homosexuality or fornication. The reasons for the honour killings could be as trivial as not serving a meal on time! Women who had allegedly brought dishonour were often raped, in order to humiliate them further. They were also sometimes sexually assaulted before being put to death by male family members, often cousins or uncles. It is therefore obvious that honour killings originate from patriarchal control of the most pernicious kind.

According to the United Nations report, five thousand honour killings take place every year around the world. The average age of these victims is twenty-three. Of these victims, the majority are daughters and sisters of their murderers, about one quarter are wives and girlfriends, and the rest include nieces, mothers, aunts and even uncles.

That daughters and sisters top the list of murder victims is horrifying and revealing. What comes to light at once is the abuse of authority by a dominant family member. A warning usually precedes the killing, followed by confinement and other types of retribution that a parent or older brother considers justified and honourable. Of the family members involved in these punishments, fathers figure significantly, accounting for one third of the murderers. Brothers are also involved in a significant way, especially in Western countries where immigrant communities have held on to their traditional beliefs and practices. These women have obviously offended the male family member greatly and the ultimate punishment–that of taking the offender's life–must therefore be inflicted.

Thus honour killings are most prevalent in societies that are still patriarchal. This includes countries of the Middle East, Bangladesh and India. Honour killings also take place in Western countries. Recent times have seen a rise in such killings but the perpetrators belong to Middle Eastern or South Asian backgrounds. In India, honour killings occur most often in Punjab, Haryana, Uttar Pradesh and Bihar. The most common reason is women marrying against the wishes of their family members.

Such crimes committed in Sikh and Hindu communities in the states of Punjab and Haryana over "wrong" marriage decisions are a manifestation of cultural practices that have existed for centuries. Societies in Haryana and Punjab are still quite patriarchal; the eldest male member of the family commands everyone's respect. Whether it pertains to decisions of matrimony or the education of girls or the places they can go or the people they can associate with, such decisions are still made by the elders of the family, especially the elder males. The patriarch, in other words, holds complete sway over the lives and destinies of the younger members, particularly the women of the family. Older women have sometimes been murdered for not bringing enough of a dowry into the village.

In recent times in the West, the majority of honour killings have involved Muslims. This puts Islamic values once again under scrutiny, and a possible link needs to be examined between Islamic mores and these murders. Ultra-orthodox Islam prescribes the segregation and veiling of women. Furthermore, Islam assigns men the task of enforcing sexual norms, through punishment if necessary.

According to this view, a woman must not associate with strange men, as that may lead to immorality and promiscuity. Gender roles are to be strictly demarcated. Women seen as flouting these social, cultural and sexual norms ought to be brought into line, according to the fundamentalists. Men must not hesitate to exercise their authority over women if it is threatened, or else they would come to be perceived as weak men. In extreme cases, the only way for them to demonstrate their ultimate authority over women is to kill them; this is the only way they can regain their lost honour. This is how the patriarchs prove to the community that no matter what the women do in the short term, it is the men who ultimately control their lives. While honour killings can and do occur in other patriarchal communities, it is sharia's emphasis on regulating sexuality that makes the incidence of honour-based violence far more likely among fundamentalist Muslims.

Consider sharia's punishment for adultery: stoning to death. This is not a Quranic punishment. However, the idea behind the actual Quranic punishment–one hundred lashes–is that men and women who commit adultery must be punished in a manner that can certainly result in death, though it does not necessarily. In my opinion, those who commit honour killings are somewhere deep in their psyche governed by this notion that violating sexual norms needs to be rewarded with death and degradation.

Let me state clearly that nowhere does the Quran or hadith imply that the honour of the father, husband, brother or son must be protected by killing a female offender in the family. Islam does not prescribe such extreme retribution.

Unveiled:

However, the Quran prescribes certain codes of sexual and moral conduct that are assigned to Muslim men to enforce. Verse 4:34 of the Quran states that husbands can beat their wives if they flout moral rules. As for Islam's punishment for adultery, though it must be administered after due process of law, few perpetrators of honour killings would ever take that into consideration.

A first step toward solving this problem would be to attack such attitudes openly. We must ask what feeds this culture of honour and punishment. Is it gossip? Is it the need for social and religious acceptance, or is it a combination of these and other reasons? Secondly, it is now time to call a spade a spade. The murders of the Shafia sisters, Aqsa Parvez and other victims of Islamist fury are honour killings–not "customary" killings or domestic violence. We must use appropriate words to describe the crime and the pathology that drives it. The link between the crime and patriarchal notions of honour is unmistakable.

In the West some apologists try to dissociate honour killings from fundamentalist Islam. All sorts of definitions that fail to do justice to the crime are offered, such as "domestic violence". Some obfuscate in this way because they fear Islamist groups. Others, notably left-leaning multiculturalists, believe in showing deference to subcultures within Canada, despite the rampant abuse of women within these communities. They therefore reject certain words deemed culturally charged.

Furthermore, these liberals promote the view that such murders occur in all religious and ethnic communities. But in trying to appear tolerant of diversity in Canada, they also unwittingly condone various misogynistic practices within these communities. One example of such equivocation is the Canadian Council of Muslim Women's stand on honour killings. The organization's position paper reads:

"CCMW's position is that defining murder by the rationale for killing diminishes the death of the woman and shifts the focus onto the perpetrator. Our argument is that in Canada no murder of a woman should be categorized by the rationale provided by the murderer, or by society itself, whether it be a so-called honour killing or a crime of passion. CCMW uses the term customary killing for this type of abhorrent crime, although this term is also not ideal, as we believe there is no honour in killing."[1]

Calling honour killings "customary" unnecessarily evades the cultural issue. The term does not serve the purpose of pinpointing the motives behind such barbaric crimes. The CCMW's position appears to be an attempt to escape any criticism that might come its way from Islamist circles who wish to dissociate the issue of honour killings from fundamentalist expressions of Islam.

Another person I communicated with through email objected to the term "honour killings" by suggesting that the term "honour" is not right to describe a dishonourable act. While such a reaction is understandable, it is important to classify the crime appropriately by using proper terminology. I therefore prefer the term "honour killing" because it links the motive to the crime clearly. It is imperative to call such crimes "honour killings" rather than simply "murder" or "domestic abuse" or "customary killings". Such labels would in fact endorse the Islamist perspective on the issue. They have always sought to discard the term "honour killing" in order to prevent any link being made between the crime and their very puritanical and punitive brand of Islam.

The Conservative government is therefore right in calling honour killings barbaric. It must now go a step further and legislate strict penalties against the crime. Too many innocent lives are at stake. Young Muslim women are often victims of beatings, confinement and abuse. Canada needs stricter laws to prevent tragedies in the name of honour. We can further help by being more aware of social trends in our communities. The concept of honour is rampant in some segments of Muslim Canadian society. Many of our neighbours, close friends and relatives who have emigrated from Middle Eastern or South Asian lands continue to cling to the notion. Patriarchal families feel threatened by the freedoms of the West, which exacerbates the culture of honour. When patriarchal families move to countries like Canada, they often impose even greater restrictions on their daughters because they fear that the chances of their daughters going astray are much greater amid Western freedoms. Verbal threats, physical abuse, removal of privileges and other punitive measures are often the lot of girls affected by this oppressive culture of honour and shame. A woman I know once told me she had warned her daughter that if the young girl ever received a phone call from a boy, the mother would break her legs.

I have discussed this troubling issue with prominent feminist Phyllis Chesler, who has done a lot of work on honour killings. She states:

"Worldwide, fifty-eight percent of the victims were murdered for being "too Western" and/or for resisting or disobeying cultural and religious expectations. The accusation of being "too Western" was the exact language used by the perpetrator or perpetrators. Being "too Western" meant being seen as too independent, not subservient enough, refusing to wear varieties of Islamic clothing (including forms of the veil), wanting an advanced education and a career, having non-Muslim (or non-Sikh or non-Hindu) friends or boyfriends, refusing to marry one's first cousin, wanting to choose one's own husband, choosing a socially "inferior" or non-Muslim (or non-Sikh or non-Hindu) husband; or leaving an abusive husband. There were statistically significant regional differences for this motive. For example, in North America, ninety-one percent of victims were murdered for being "too Western" as compared to a smaller but still substantial number (seventy-one percent) in Europe. In comparison, only forty-three percent of victims were killed for this reason in the Muslim world."[2]

Immigration, law enforcement, and religious authorities must all be included in any campaign to halt the curse of honour killings. Additionally, shelters for oppressed girls and women should be swiftly established. The law must also protect young Muslim girls who are often lured back home by their family members. The staff at these shelters must prevent the girls from being returned to any abusive home. Something similar to a federal witness protection program for these vulnerable girls should be created, as it already has in Britain. Safe foster family networks should replace existing family networks when they are the source of the threat.

The government of Canada must convey zero tolerance for such crimes and this must be effectively communicated to Muslim, Sikh and Hindu immigrants and citizens. Furthermore, honour killings must be treated separately from domestic violence, and perpetrators must be publicly shamed. There is a fundamental difference between honour crimes and other types of domestic violence. The fundamental difference is that honour crimes are usually premeditated; they are planned by families. Domestic violence often occurs on the spur of the moment, but honour killings almost never do.

Western judicial systems and governments have recently begun to address this problem. In 2006, a Danish court convicted nine members of a clan for the honour murder of Ghazala Khan. In 2009, a German court sentenced a father to life in prison for having ordered his son to murder his sister for the family honour, while the twenty-year-old son was sentenced to nine and a half years. In another case a British court, with the help of testimony from the victim's mother and fiancé, convicted a father of a ten-year-old honour murder after the crime was reclassified; and the Canadian government has finally been informing new immigrants of Western expectations.

Muslims emigrating to Canada and the United States need to acknowledge that their children, especially daughters, are human beings with independent minds and normal aspirations. It is understandable to worry about the conduct of our children. It is our right as parents to guide our children and even admonish them at times. But no one has the right to injure and kill daughters due to medieval notions of family honour or disdain for Western society. It is high time patriarchal cultures treated their women with compassion and humanity. Parents and guardians of these oppressed women and girls need to be encouraged to rethink their priorities, because culture and tradition cannot be offered as excuses. They must realize that the happiness and sanity of their daughters are more important than the idle gossip of friends and acquaintances. They must shun medieval notions of honour that have caused so much despair in these patriarchal communities.

The Sharia Debate

I was fresh out of university in 1982, and gainfully employed at Lahore's prestigious Pakistan Administrative Staff College as a junior research associate. That was the year General Mohammad Ziaul Haqq, Pakistan's Islamist military dictator, introduced a controversial law that would render women vulnerable to murder and violence because their *diyat* (blood money) would amount to half that of a male victim of murder. It was also around that time that the Women's Action Forum of Pakistan began to protest the discrimination embodied in Ziaul Haqq's retrogressive sharia laws. A woman's value was indeed only half that of a man's, according to this view. I was now beginning to see sharia in action for the first time.

The religious climate of the country had changed from somewhat secular to staunchly pious. Centuries of British colonial rule had dampened and fused the religious identity of Muslims, Hindus and other ethnic, religious and cultural groups in pre-partition India. The religion Muslims practiced in the subcontinent under the Raj was a syncretistic faith that combined elements of Hindu shrine worship and Islamic monotheism. Now the Muslim people of an independent Pakistan were slowly beginning to rediscover their religious identity. They were reverting to a more pristine understanding of their faith. They were now more receptive to religious laws and they found in Ziaul Haqq an ardent proponent of this revived religious insularity.

 A group of women, including human rights activist Asma Jahangir, her lawyer sister Hina Jilani and the Women's Action Forum, organized a protest against the injustice inherent in the new "blood money" laws. Blood money is offered as recompense for murder under sharia law. A family can accept the

51

money in lieu of the death sentence that the perpetrator might have received. As a young university graduate, I participated in that protest, carrying banners in front of the Punjab governor's house in Lahore. Little did I know that I was being photographed and would appear on the front page of a Lahore daily, along with other protesters. One of my colleagues spotted me in the picture, and reminded me that, as an employee of a government institution, I was prohibited from participating in political protests. My colleague assured me he would stay quiet about my little political adventure. Luckily no one else noticed me in the photograph and my transgression went unnoticed by government authorities.

The rationale under sharia for prescribing *diyat* or blood money is simply to compensate the family for any financial hardship incurred due to murder. A man, as the breadwinner, contributes income to the household. A woman in a traditional Muslim family makes no such contribution. Therefore when a woman dies, her loss is not felt as deeply by the family as a man's, at least from an economic standpoint.

The disadvantage of such a law of course is that women are left more vulnerable to violence and murder. Furthermore, in this day and age, a woman is often the sole breadwinner for her family. Ziaul Haqq, by enacting such a medieval law, was ignoring the realities of contemporary life. Law should not discriminate based on archaic gender roles when the circumstances and responsibilities of men and women in modern societies can be so comparable. The law should not discriminate based on gender at all.

Perhaps the most baleful development under Ziaul Haqq's policy of Islamization was the enactment of the *hadood* (plural of *hadd*) laws. These were laws based on the Quranic concept of God's "limits". The "limits" included crimes like murder and theft and offences like adultery and fornication. Under the new laws, men and women convicted of adultery or fornication would have to suffer the Quranic punishment of one hundred lashes. Granted, these laws and their negative consequences were debated openly in Pakistan at the time. Many reformist religious scholars had already warned the military dictator about the adverse ramifications of such legislation, especially for women and religious minorities. However, Ziaul Haqq capitulated to the clerics and feudal landlords by enacting these laws on adultery and fornication.

Coupled with the *hadood* laws were the new regulations on testimony. Women were now barred from testifying in courts of law for *hadood* cases. That meant they could not testify against their rapists. The court would require four "Muslim adult males of good repute" to prove a charge of rape. Such a preposterous condition naturally made rape nearly impossible to prove. In fact, any woman bringing forward a charge of rape could instead be charged with adultery.

Women were now afraid to bring charges of rape against perpetrators lest they themselves be hauled before the court. Men, on the other hand, began to feel empowered. A number of very high profile rape cases would emerge in Pakistan over the next several years after the introduction of the infamous *hadood* ordinance that criminalized adultery while ignoring rape as an independent crime under the law.

One case that caught my attention in the mid-eighties was that of thirteen-year-old Safia Bibi. The girl was prosecuted for adultery because she became pregnant as a result of rape. The perpetrators, father and son, were both acquitted for lack of evidence under the new regulations on testimony. On the other hand, the girl's pregnancy was admitted as proof of adultery.

Safia Bibi, a poor peasant's daughter, was an employee at the house of her landlord, where she worked from morning till night. She discharged her daily domestic chores relentlessly, despite being vision-impaired. In Pakistan domestic employment is not regulated and is akin to slavery; servants toil from morning till night in return for a monthly pittance. They are perpetually scolded, ridiculed and demeaned by their employers. In many respects they are considered worse than animals. Such was Safia Bibi's lot.

Some reports suggest she was sixteen years old at the time of the rape. Her rapists were from the prosperous feudal class of Pakistan. Feudal landlords in Pakistan often consider themselves the lords and masters of their impoverished employees and feel no compunction in playing with their emotions or even their very lives.

The rape itself was only the beginning of the suffering for the nearly blind Safia Bibi. When she took her complaint to authorities, they instead charged her with adultery, because the victim could not produce the four adult male witnesses of good repute to prove the crime under Ziaul Haqq's new Islamic laws. For their testimony to be considered valid, the four flawless men would have had to witness the act of penetration. Who in his right mind would commit rape in the presence of four adult Muslim males of good standing?

Sure enough, instead of convicting the rapists, the sharia court awarded the girl the punishment of fifteen lashes in public, three years' imprisonment and a fine of a thousand rupees. The Quranic punishment would have been one hundred lashes, but in view of her tender age, the court magnanimously decided to reduce the punishment: an act that mocked true compassion.

This was a young girl from an underprivileged family. Had it not been for women's human rights groups in Pakistan, the victim would have met a very tragic end. She would have been publicly shamed. Her reputation would have been forever tarnished and she would very possibly have been the victim of rape again, as women who are accused of turpitude are legitimate targets for rape. Thankfully, human rights agencies and women's rights groups were informed of Safia's plight. Needless to say, the Women's Action Forum also jumped to help Safia. After considerable public outrage, the girl was acquitted. Safia later gave birth to a child who died.

The victim's anguish had no end. Safia's violation had tainted her reputation in a country that places high value on a family's honour. Her poor peasant father was initially afraid to bring rape charges on the perpetrators. Since Safia was allegedly a minor at the time of the rape, it was her father who needed to take her rapists to court. They of course responded by saying the girl was of loose character. It was fear of such counter-accusations that had kept the family from going to court initially.

Her attackers were not convicted. Their crime could not be proved because of the sharia requirement of four adult male witnesses. The onus was on the accuser entirely. In the end, Safia Bibi's case was closed on "technical grounds": no redress, no justice and naturally no compensation for the victim.

This was Pakistan under the new sharia laws: the weak and vulnerable were left even more marginalized and victimized. I could immediately empathize with Safia Bibi. What if this were me? What if I were born into an impoverished family where I was left at the mercy of my employees? What if I had endured such a crime, with the law squarely on the side of the men who violated me?

Many such draconian sharia measures were being implemented in Pakistan at that time. Ziaul Haqq passed these so-called *hadood* ordinances, whereby men and women could be charged with adultery and punished accordingly. It turned out that the majority of those convicted under these laws were women, as sharia law made absolutely no distinction between rape and adultery.

Soon, I would learn that Ahmedi Begum, Majidah Abdullah and other women from Pakistani society's poorest segments would become victims of similar rapes. And it was these same women, rather than their attackers, who would end up in prison. The rapists could continue their attacks with impunity. There was nothing in the new laws on witnessing or distinctions between rape and adultery that would benefit women in any way. These in fact became some of the most vulnerable women in the world.

The fundamentalist wave in the country would see other atrocities being committed in Islam's name. In 1994 the tragic fate of Zainab Noor, a poor woman from a rural area, hit the newsstands. This poor woman had simply sought permission from her husband to visit her family. According to sharia law, she was required to seek this permission from her lord and master, her husband.

Tragically, her husband happened to be a local cleric with his own rather puritanical understanding of sharia.

I visited Zainab in hospital, accompanied by my nephew. He was as distraught as I was to see the woman in agony. The poor woman lay in the hospital bed, curled up with the pain her husband had inflicted on her. He had taken a burning rod and inserted it up her vagina because she pleaded with him to let her visit her family. Her insides were completely burnt and destroyed. She would have to be fed through a tube for the rest of her life, the doctor said. Then Prime Minister, the since deceased Benazir Bhutto, donated considerable money for Zainab Noor's treatment, under much public pressure. Imam Sharif, Zainab's husband, was convicted of the crime—once again due to public pressure. In Pakistan men would normally go unpunished for physically chastising their wives, because sharia law sanctions it.

Zainab was hardly four feet ten inches tall, and it seemed she had been underfed. Her son, six at the time, was too young to understand what had happened to his mother. Zainab hardly said a word to me. But the expression on her face said it all. She was in agony and despair. Her husband was supposed to have protected her. He almost killed her instead. The poor woman was finally sent to London for treatment but she returned after undergoing surgery and having a colostomy bag fitted for life.

I begged Zainab's mother never to send the woman back to her husband. She was twenty-four at the time of the attack. The mother assured me that her daughter would not be returned to this monster. I was still afraid that these were empty assurances, as divorce in countries like Pakistan carries an enormous stigma. When girls leave their parents' home to join the husband's family, they are told never to come back, to return only upon a funeral pyre and to endure any and every hardship that comes their way with dignity and forbearance. Social structures in Pakistan tend to be terribly oppressive for women in their husband's family homes. I feared that Zainab would be sent back because of these social considerations. Thankfully, after following her trail since I visited her, I am told that she currently resides in a women's hostel in Islamabad. Her son is now grown up.

Imam Sharif, Zainab's husband, is out of prison. He was initially convicted by the Suppression of Terrorist Activities Court on February 19, 1994 on three counts and was sentenced to thirty years' imprisonment. He was additionally required to compensate his wife financially upon leaving prison.

He appealed this sentence. Upon hearing of Imam Sharif's appeal, the Lahore High Court commuted the trial court judgment to the effect that the sentence would run concurrently, not consecutively. In Pakistan life in prison is fourteen years. Sharif has since apologized for the brutality inflicted on his wife, but Zainab's dignity can never be restored or her injury rectified.

The Quran permits men to use force to make their wives comply with their wishes. These wishes have been interpreted to mean anything that may suit a husband's fancy. While many translations of the Quran recommend that husbands beat their wives only "lightly", it is difficult for men to control their rage in a fit of fury. The fact that sharia permits wife battery in any form, to any degree and for any reason is intolerable. Concerns about women's safety in such situations have too often been proved justified. Zainab Noor suffered the effects of such brutality, and other documented evidence show that beatings often lead to permanent injury. Yet any incident of a man hitting a woman is abuse. How can the slightest episode of it ever be tolerated?

Domestic abuse is not confined to wife-battery. Even in Canada, girls are beaten routinely by their fathers and brothers to keep them in check and in line with the sharia requirement that they not date or associate with boys. Wives are often beaten into submission as well over issues of parental control. In families where the governing force is sharia, the dynamics never favour women.

I married my husband in 1984. The process of Islamization of Pakistan's laws had continued since 1977, when Pakistan's Islamist military dictator Ziaul Haqq came to power. He enjoyed tremendous popularity with the masses. In 1982 he conducted a farcical nationwide referendum to the effect that if the Pakistani people wanted Pakistan to be an Islamic Republic, they should vote for him. This was really a cynical ploy to lend some validity to his military rule. It was also successful, for who would dare question Islamic rule? So it was that the wily dictator's rule would last eleven years, till Ziaul Haqq was killed in a military plane crash in 1988.

Our marriage was solemnized against the backdrop of Ziaul Haqq's Islamic laws. It seemed that the Pakistani people, after centuries of forgetting their religious precepts and practices, were waking up to a militant and fundamentalist brand of Islam. It was then that I was made aware of my predicament as a Muslim woman living in Pakistan. My brother-in-law, a prominent Pakistani lawyer, informed me that in order for me to secure myself the right to divorce, I would need to have it stipulated in the Muslim marriage contract or *nikah* document. He brought this up with my mother, who was completely averse to the idea. It was bad luck to talk about divorce when entering into a marriage bond, she thought. Nonetheless, my brother-in-law persisted and said that I should still have that "delegated right to divorce my husband if things did not work out between the two of us."

I realized immediately that without such a clause, I would not be entering the union as an equal. Even with the clause, my husband had the unilateral right to divorce me whereas I had access only to a "delegated right of divorce, and that too if the parties did not find it distasteful to include it in the *nikah* document." This was sharia law in action, and this time it had a direct bearing on my life.

My mother reluctantly requested the local imam to speak to my then fiancé about agreeing to the condition. My husband still recalls, with much amusement, how the imam approached him rather gingerly before opening up conversation on the issue. He recalls how my husband simply laughed it off by saying that no, he had no objection, that he would never force a woman to stay in the marriage if she felt compelled to leave. Thankfully, my husband was enlightened enough to accept the logic of the *haqq tafweez,* or delegated right of divorce. My brother-in-law was finally successful in procuring the delegated right of divorce for me.

But most men and women are unequal when entering unions. They are also unequal when these unions end in divorce. This was all true under sharia law as it was understood and being applied in Pakistan. But I was young and getting married. There was a whole life for me to look forward to, and I was not to think much about inherent inequalities between the rights of men and women until much later.

It was in 2003 that I would investigate these issues in detail again. Here in Ontario, religious courts had been functioning for some time where divorce, custody and alimony cases were being dispensed under sharia law. The rationale was that these courts were faster, whereas regular civil Ontario courts had a tremendous backlog of unresolved divorce and custody cases.

Religions can shape culture and society, and Muslims who subscribe to fundamentalist expressions of the faith often pursue the agenda of institutional change in Western societies. The move to introduce faith-based arbitration was one such example. It took me a while to understand the issues behind the raging debate. It seemed all Muslim organizations were somehow involved, with the majority of course supporting sharia. The only two organizations opposed to sharia courts were the Muslim Canadian Congress and the Canadian Council of Muslim Women.

At first I considered the brouhaha over sharia misplaced and perhaps an expression of anti-Islam sentiment. Why the uproar? The Jewish *beit dins* had been functioning in Canada as well, and no one had objected to those. Aha! It must be the West's inveterate hatred of Islam. The word "Islamophobia" was heard many times during those days. Why was there so much suspicion of

Muslims, of their beliefs, practices and culture? Sharia after all only meant that Muslims could settle their domestic disputes in a quicker, more efficient manner. These would include cases involving alimony, divorce and custody of children. But it would soon become apparent to me that the ramifications of sharia dispensations on these issues would not be as benign or equitable as some would have us believe. I recalled how my own marriage contract could have placed me on a very unequal footing. I recalled how Zainab and Safia were treated.

The sharia debate erupted in Ontario in 2003, the year after my husband and I performed the Hajj, the pilgrimage to Mecca. I was then president of the Islamic outfit Muslims Against Terrorism. Syed Soharwardy had founded this group in response to radicalism in the Islamic world. He wished to counter this trend through a more benign interpretation of Quranic verses. I had received an email from him soon after 9/11, requesting that I take charge of the Mississauga chapter of the organization.

In my naivety, I had thought that this was the best way to counter radicalism. I was soon to learn that the organization was more of a Muslim advocacy group than what its name suggested, an organization to counter extremism and radicalism among Muslims. Furthermore, I found that I could not for long simply be a "Muslim Against Terrorism"; much more had to be done to bring about reform among Muslims. It was the sharia controversy that finally put things into perspective for me. Syed Soharwardy soon began to endorse barrister Syed Mumtaz Ali's call to introduce sharia law in Ontario. I found myself at odds with much of what Muslims Against Terrorism stood for from that point on.

At that time, I also began to get involved with the activities of the Muslim Canadian Congress, the liberal and progressive organization co-founded by author and activist Tarek Fatah. I initially agreed to join its board of directors and found it to be far more suited to my religious sensibilities than Muslims Against Terrorism had ever been. I therefore parted from Muslims Against Terrorism and joined the MCC in 2004. I have been an active member of the organization since that time and also served as its president from 2006 to 2009.

Needless to say, my main issue with sharia was its treatment of women. Parallel religious courts threatened the rights of Muslim women. Even though proponents of sharia assured Muslim women that they would have access to Canadian courts in case they felt short-changed by sharia provisions, I knew their access to the Canadian justice system would be denied for various sociological reasons. Once again, the issue of patriarchal control would surface. Women would be beaten into submission by their husbands in order to prevent them from seeking redress in Canadian courts. Beating was allowed under sharia. The biggest threat to equitable treatment of women in sharia courts would involve custody and alimony cases.

All this was part of the larger issue of whether Islam was indeed misogynistic. Islam is most often criticized for two reasons: violence and the status of Muslim women. Sharia permits polygamy and concubinage. It also prescribes unequal inheritance shares, and in some circumstances wife-beating. Zainab Noor had been a victim of wife-battery gone awry. But sharia discriminates against women on countless other issues as well. It awards unfair custody rights to men and absolves them of long-term alimony obligations.

During that time I was asked to provide assistance to a young Muslim woman fighting a custody battle. She belonged to a minority sect within Islam. For safety reasons I will use a fictional name for her. Simi had been ostracized by the community for defying the orders of the then spiritual head of the community. Her in-laws had asserted their right to custody of the two-year-old son. The young woman insisted on custody and was willing to take the fight all the way. Her main fear was that she would be excommunicated from her faith community for defying the spiritual leader's orders. In Islam, a mother is entitled to custody of her son for the first two years of his life and of her daughter until she reaches puberty. The custody then automatically goes to the father. Divine law was against this poor girl, as was the social fabric of the religious community she belonged to. In the end, local lawyers were consulted and Simi was awarded custody.

Although the Quran on occasion accords some rights to women, it also clearly places men in charge of women in a great many situations. Verse 4:34 of the Quran states:

Men are the protectors and sustainers of women because God has given the one more (strength) than the other, and because they support them from their means, therefore the devout women are righteously obedient and guard themselves (in the husband's absence) what God would have them guard. As for those women from whom you fear disloyalty and ill-conduct, admonish them (first), refuse to share their beds (next), and last beat them (lightly). But, if they return to obedience, seek not against them means of annoyance, for God is most High, Great. (Quran 4: 34).

For fundamentalist Muslims (and I have debated these issues with many of them) this verse summarizes the status of women in Islam as being subordinate to men. It goes so far as to say that women must be physically chastised if they disobey their husbands. But ask Miriam Abushaban, a twenty-two-year-old Concordia University student, if she believes Islam oppresses her. Chances are, she and most other burka-clad women will say no and that, in fact, they enjoy a very privileged position under the benign umbrella of Islam.

Dr. Riffat Hassan, Professor of Theology at the University of Louisville, Kentucky, is my maternal aunt and a well-known modernist theologian of Islam. She believes her religion does not discriminate against women, but maintains that the fault lies with flawed translations of the Quran. The conviction that Islam in fact favours women is therefore quite prevalent among Muslims of all persuasions, be they nominally conservative or moderate. This apparent contradiction can be explained by the fact that there is an entire industry among the more fundamentalist and conservative devotees dedicated to promoting and defending orthodox Islam's position on women. Its purveyors work tirelessly to prove that sharia is in fact highly protective of them, that it elevates them, liberates them, and gives them a position in society which Western women can neither dream of nor fathom.

During my encounters with conservative Muslims I also came across the following comment by Joanne Bailey, a thirty-year-old British convert to Islam:

> "Contrary to what most people think, Islam doesn't oppress me; it lets me be the person that I was all along. Now I'm so much more content and grateful for the things I've got. A few months ago, I got engaged to a Muslim solicitor I met on a training course. He has absolutely no problem with my career, but I do agree with the Islamic perspective on the traditional roles for men and women. I want to look after my husband and children, but I also want my independence. I'm proud to be British and I'm proud to be Muslim–and I don't see them as conflicting in any way."[1]

It was women like Bailey who amazed me the most. For me they posed the greatest challenge to any reform within Islam. They had completely bought into the rationale that explains away inequalities between the rights of men and women. If Western-educated women could not see the inherent discrimination, what could one expect from poor and illiterate women? To my utter dismay, many of the proponents of sharia in Ontario were women!

Fundamentalist female theologians like Farhat Hashmi had a profound impact on these pro-sharia women. They would gladly endorse Bailey's view that the roles of men and women in society are separate, unequal and complementary and must be kept that way for the overall good of society. Hashmi went so far as to urge her "Muslim sisters" to allow their husbands to marry a second, third or fourth time to benefit other "sisters". She asserted she was a feminist, looking out for the interest of Muslim women. I heard these comments at a lecture Farhat Hashmi delivered in 2004. After the lecture, I challenged Hashmi on her opinions. She calmly responded by saying the ultimate authority is that of the husband's and no matter what the differences, his views must prevail over hers.

This was a woman endorsing the subservient role of Muslim women. I knew that polygamous reality was different from Hashmi's idealistic view of women sharing a husband. The prophet Mohammad's wives often fought for his attention, sometimes with unpleasant consequences. According to a well-known hadith, the wives of the prophet formed two rival camps, led by Ayesha and Zainab Bint Jahsh, both envied for their extraordinary beauty. Ayesha frequently expressed jealousy for Zainab as the prophet often lingered at Zainab's quarters when it was her turn to entertain him. As a result, Ayesha plotted with members of her camp to convince Mohammad that he invariably returned with bad breath after visiting Zainab because she fed him *maghafir* (a foul-smelling gum). This led to friction among the wives and a rebuke from Allah that the prophet would have to pack them off if they continued to misbehave.

The value system that sharia proponents like Soharwardy, Mumtaz Ali, Bailey and Hashmi were proposing was a matter of grave concern to me because of how sharia oppressed women. I disagree with scholars like John Esposito who claim that the conservatives and fundamentalists of Islam constitute the fringe and can therefore be ignored. He suggests they are too few to do any harm. It may very well be true that the extremists constitute a minority among Muslims, but it is these very individuals who are calling the shots and driving the agendas. It is this small but highly vocal minority that wants to "Islamize" the West, and it is these diehards who perpetually demand outrageous faith accommodations that circumscribe the scope and purpose of Canada's democratic institutions. A classic example is the demand by Islamic organizations to have any criticism of religion declared blasphemous. Such a law would eventually be introduced under sharia. I know that Pakistan's minority communities have already suffered from the effects of blasphemy laws. Needless to say, meeting such demands in the West would severely curtail the right to freedom of speech, the cornerstone of Western liberal democracies. Author and journalist Mark Steyn has already been taken to task in Canada by the conservative Canadian Islamic Congress for his book *America Alone.*

Polygamy would be allowed under sharia. In the GTA alone, there are reportedly one hundred Muslim men who are in polygamous unions. The law in Ontario recognizes polygamous unions contracted abroad, even though polygamy is not legal in Canada. The infamous Mr Shafia, who killed his three young daughters, was himself in a polygamous marriage. His first wife produced no children. His second wife was of course convicted as an accomplice in the murder of her three young daughters and their stepmother.

Unveiled:

Rona Amir Mohammad, the unfortunate first wife, had been calling relatives in the United States to tell them how stifling her life had become in Canada. She was a glorified maid, cooking and cleaning for her husband's new family. She was insulted, ridiculed and demeaned by the younger wife. This was typical of the kinds of domestic politics and power structures polygamy engenders under sharia law.

After witnessing such horrendous effects of sharia law in action, I simply could not defend the introduction of sharia courts in Canada. A local imam by the name of Essa Adam had passed a rather ominous judgment on me for opposing sharia. He told me I was "out of the fold of Islam" if I opposed sharia. This judgment could mean a death sentence against me, because anyone who apostatizes from the faith can be a prime target for execution.

The negative effects of sharia are not confined to women. They can have an impact on anyone who is seen to oppose Islamic values, ethics and beliefs. The Muslim Canadian Congress, an organization I had joined by then, led a valiant campaign to ban faith-based arbitration. Tarek Fatah, Munir Pervaiz, Hasan Mahmud, Niaz Salimi and others wrote articles and met with politicians to warn them of the dangers of sharia courts. Thankfully, on September 11 2005, Premier Dalton McGuinty declared that all faith-based arbitration would be banned in Ontario and that there would simply be one law for everyone.

The Burka Debate

In 2002 my husband and I performed the Hajj, the annual pilgrimage to Mecca. The view of the Kaaba at the centre of the grand mosque in Mecca was inspiring, as was the religious zeal among the two million pilgrims to the holiest city of Islam. But what struck me most about my visit to Mecca was the plight of the burka-clad women in the sweltering heat of the Saudi desert sun. These were women who were covered from head to toe–literally. Even their hands were concealed, covered in black gloves lest the lustful eyes of foreign men might get enticed by their beauty or tantalizing "sexual" appeal. I had assumed that every part of a woman's body is considered a sexual object in patriarchal Muslim societies, and the spectacle of these fully covered women confirmed my observations. This was Saudi Arabia: the cradle of Islam, and the unofficial but unchallenged religious capital of the Islamic world. In fact Saudi and Wahhabi ideas were being exported elsewhere in the world, and I even encountered them frequently right here in Canada.

At a social gathering organized by a devoutly religious friend, I met a woman by the name of Sabiha, who explained that Islam indeed prescribed the burka. She argued that a Muslim woman's garb must not reveal the color of her skin or the shape of her body. Her outer garments must therefore be loose enough to hide her contours, and dark enough to conceal the color of her skin. She noted with dismay that the burka could not conceal the height of a woman, but that was something she could not help and Allah would forgive women if the burka failed to conceal their height. What could I do except shake my head in despair and disbelief? Why this preoccupation with women's bodies and why the pathological need to conceal them from public gaze? Why is the onus entirely on women to ensure archaic male-defined propriety?

I live in a middle class neighbourhood in suburban Mississauga. Behind the single-unit residential homes, there is a complex of low-income housing where many of the new Middle Eastern and South Asian immigrants reside. I do not recall seeing even one niqabi woman prior to 9/11 in that complex populated by Pakistani and Middle Eastern immigrants. However, now I encounter several, and only within a span of a decade. Women entering and leaving that complex either fully or partially cover their faces. This proliferation of the burka and niqab worries me greatly. What sort of a society are we allowing here in Canada? Should we accept the marginalization of Muslim women in Canada? Have we gone too far in our policy of multiculturalism? Can all cultures be treated with respect, even if they oppress women?

As a Muslim woman I dread the spread of the burka and the Wahhabi ideology that drives it. While I am not overly concerned about the hijab, a garment that does not conceal a woman's identity or hinder her movements, the burka disturbs and offends me greatly.

Rooted in Wahhabi culture, the burka is a political tool to subjugate women, ensuring that they remain subservient to the demands and whims of the kind of men who stipulate such rules for them. In this regard, Wahhabis often appeal to Western notions of freedom, asserting that the state "has no business in the wardrobes of the nation." In Canada we are concerned about individual liberties. Our charter guarantees citizens freedom of religion, a notion greatly abused by religious fundamentalists. Is the right to wear the burka a right to be exercised to the exclusion of other rights? Can one still call for a burka ban in Canada despite Canada's individual freedoms and democratic tradition?

I became intensely involved in the burka debate soon after I took charge of the Muslim Canadian Congress, an organization which stands for secular governance and full equality of Muslim women. The year was 2006, and the time was ripe for an honest debate on the place of the burka in modern Canadian society. However, there were many issues to consider before formally considering a campaign to outlaw the oppressive garb. Burning issues were the constitutionality of a burka ban, the right of women to choose what to wear, religious freedoms, the threat to public security, the physical health of burka-clad women, patriarchal control, political Islam and how the burka is a tool in the hands of individuals with an indisputably political agenda. No doubt a ban on the burka would curtail the rights of some Muslim citizens of Canada. But what was to be gained? I pondered these questions at length and decided that on balance, a burka ban would greatly help Muslim women who were being suppressed and marginalized by husbands, fathers, brothers or even sons.

I proceeded to call for a burka ban in Canada with the assistance of the MCC's board of directors and its founder, Tarek Fatah. In a letter to the Canadian government, the MCC cited concerns over the security of the public, the safety of burka-clad women as well as the resultant marginalization of veiled women in Canadian society. As expected, the MCC met with opposition from fundamentalist groups as well as from non-Muslims who embrace an uncompromising form of multiculturalism or contemporary notions of feminism. They argued that a burka ban would restrict the choices of women who wear the niqab or burka and contravene Canada's Charter of Rights and Freedoms.

The defenders of the burka included some fundamentalists with a decidedly political agenda. Dr. Farhat Hashmi is a female theologian who runs a religious school in Mississauga. She continually and aggressively markets the garb to potential converts, insisting the burka is required by Islam. Women must aspire to it, as it represents the highest level of piety a Muslim woman can attain. A female medical doctor who lives in the apartment complex behind the Sheridan Mall in Mississauga is disciple of Hashmi's. She knows that the burka is not required by Islam. I asked her why she still chose to don it. She responded by saying it was out of a desire for greater *taqwa* (piety). I knew at once that even burka-clad women were not convinced that they had to wear it; it has just become a political tool.

Shortly after calling for a burka ban, I received an email from professor Nikkie Keddie of the University of California, endorsing my view that the niqab was mainly a political tool and that it was not religiously mandated. Soon after we connected on the internet, she sent me her scholarly book entitled *Women in the Middle East: Past and Present*. According to this well-known academic the religious attire was imposed on Muslim women only gradually. Her contention was supported by history. Her book recorded that in the early periods of Islamic history, women had considerable freedom to roam unveiled. Some wore the veil as a manifestation of patriarchal mores. Additionally, Bedouin men and women were accustomed to cover their hair and face to protect themselves from the desert sun, but there was no historical evidence to support the notion that the garment was worn for religious reasons.

Prof. Keddie notes in her book that the cultural veiling of women predates Islam. She writes: "Some works on Islamic history concentrate on pre-Islamic Arabian society, but today it is widely recognized that many crucial phenomena regarding women in Islamic times arose not from Arabia but from the pre-Islamic civilizations of Southwest Asia, early conquered by Muslim armies."[1]

She further writes: "The pre-Islamic Middle East and the East European Mediterranean had various forms of veiling and seclusion, especially of elite women. Assyrian law of the late second millennium gave men proprietary rights

65

over women, exclusive divorce rights, and specified rules on veiling. High status women had to veil, while harlots and slaves were forbidden to."[2]

I now realized that Islam did not introduce or stipulate the face veil. Some historians even suggested the veil was rooted more in ancient Greek and Byzantine culture. Among these elitist cultures, women were progressively more hidden from society based on class and social standing. The underlying assumption was that noblewomen would have far more to lose if they were dishonoured; best to keep them secluded and protected. My sense is that when Islam spread to these lands, it adopted some of the local customs and restrictions. According to various historical accounts, the caliphs of Islam began to maintain large harems where women would have no contact with strange men. These harems included free women as well as concubines.

It is quite possible that Quranic injunctions on modesty, though worded quite vaguely, came to be interpreted in line with these adopted cultural practices. Women were seen as temptresses whose behaviour had to be monitored and restricted. Islamic law continued to evolve in the centuries following the prophet Mohammad's death and most certainly came to reflect medieval attitudes toward women's place in society.

But even in the eighth and ninth centuries, slaves and nomadic peoples were barred from veiling. In fact they were punished if they violated this rule because it meant they were pretending to belong to the nobility. It was as late as the thirteenth century that the Mameluke dynasty of Egypt issued a universal decree stipulating the face veil for Muslim women whenever they appeared in public. What was once a mark of aristocracy and nobility now came to be imposed universally as irrefutable religious dogma.

I could not merely rely on the opinions of others or on those of contemporary non-Muslim scholars like Keddie. I had to develop my own understanding of the issue of veiling and segregation in Islam. I embarked on a detailed study of the Quran to determine for myself what was or wasn't required. What follows are the conclusions I drew from my study of Quranic edicts.

Quranic injunctions about modesty are worded vaguely. They do not specify that women must cover their hair or face. What the Quran suggests is modesty in dress and demeanour, pure and simple. Yet ultra-conservative Muslims like Sabiha or Hashmi insist that the full veiling of women is in fact a religious requirement. They often cite ambiguously worded quotes from the Quran to dismiss valid arguments against face coverings. According to their interpretation, the verse on veiling talks about a curtain being thrown over an object or person. They insist that verse 33: 53 of the Quran, which exhorts Muslim women to draw their veils over themselves, implies that the face must be covered as well. They also suggest that the Quran talks about women covering their beauty, and that the face falls into this category. In my opinion, this ultraconservative viewpoint within Islam is inauthentic and unwarranted. According to Islamic jurisprudence, Muslims must not follow the minority interpretation. The recognized schools of Islamic jurisprudence prescribe four methods of interpretation that give shape to precept and practice. These comprise the Quran itself, the *sunnah* (the oral traditions of the prophet, called *hadith*), *ijma* (the consensus of the Muslim community on religious issues) and *qiyas* (analogy).

The most relevant to our current discussion is the third principle of Islamic jurisprudence, called *ijma* or consensus, of which there are two types. The first involves the consensus of the Muslim community, which need not include scholars. The second pertains to consensus of religious scholars. Muslims are required to follow the precepts agreed upon by a majority of scholars. Yet nowhere in the Islamic world have the scholars achieved a consensus that Islam mandates covering the face.

While scholars agree on the hijab, the head covering worn by mainstream Muslim women, no orthodox scholar with the exception of the Wahhabi sheiks believes that the Quran mandates face covering. Muslims across the world are supposed to follow the consensus of the community, giving special weight to the views of the scholars, yet the ultra-conservative prefer to advocate a minority opinion. That they choose this course further confirms that Islam is becoming manipulated.

Canada is thankfully a free country. The hijab and burka could both be outlawed in an Islamic country if the regime of that country so desired. It happened in Turkey in 1924 when Kemal Ataturk declared Turkey a republic. But this debate has been erupting in Canada, where there are inalienable freedoms to consider. Canada's Charter of Rights and Freedoms stipulates, among other things, freedom of conscience and religion, and freedom of expression. Choice of attire is perhaps a means of expression.

Therefore, even supposedly progressive Muslim groups like the Canadian Council of Muslim Women oppose a burka ban, citing the religious freedoms argument. Many believe that it is not up to the state to determine which religious practice is valid. The burka is in my view a deviant religious practice. However, the Charter acknowledges even deviant religious practice as a religious right. The whole purpose of separating religion and state is to ensure that the state maintains neutrality towards all religious practices, including ones which the mainstream may regard as abnormal. It is therefore not up to the state to determine the authenticity of a particular religious practice. If some individuals believe Islam mandates the burka or face veil, then the state must not question that religious view. This interpretation of Charter provisions would certainly confer legitimacy on the burka, even though its advocates hold a minority opinion which the Muslim majority considers deviant.

However, religious rights must be tempered. Is the right to wear a burka an absolute right, or can it be subjected to reasonable limits, and if so, what are those limits? Some deviant religious practices may be neutral or even benign, while others may be quite detrimental to society. Furthermore, some religious rights impinge on the rights of other individuals or of society in general. In this case, it is justified to place limits on them. The burka or face coverings fall into this category.

I researched section one of the Charter to further enrich my understanding of the issue. It states:

1. The Canadian Charter of Rights and Freedoms guarantees the rights and freedoms set out in it subject only to such reasonable limits prescribed by law as can be demonstrably justified in a free and democratic society.

In keeping with this provision, I would have to determine what is or isn't a reasonable limit on the practice of wearing the burka that can be "demonstrably justified" in a free and democratic society like Canada.

In 2010, France moved to ban the niqab from public spaces. Quebec also passed bill 94 that would deny public services to women in niqabs, all in the interest of ensuring equality and maximum opportunity for Muslim women. Later that year, I received an invitation to speak at the world famous Doha Debates on France's burka ban. I spoke for the motion: *This house believes France is right to ban the face veil.*

I argued that the security of the public was paramount in this debate. I asserted that the burka conceals identity. While other garments such as ski masks and balaclavas can also be used to conceal identity, their use is restricted to athletic activities conducted in areas that are specifically demarcated. Certainly, the use of any kind of face masks should be restricted in public. But the burka presents a unique problem. It is worn by a significantly larger number of individuals at all times of the day in all sorts of public spaces. People do not wear ski masks in public on a normal day. Conservative Muslim women, however, do wear the burka or niqab in public on a normal day. This makes it more likely to be abused by criminals, and it has in fact been linked to bank robberies and terrorism. Since a terrorist attack can occur anywhere, any time, we must decide whether it is more important to protect an individual's supposed right to wear the burka in public, or to reinforce the safety of other citizens. Is banning the burka therefore constitutional? We should consider some more evidence of its criminal abuse.

Burka related crimes have been on the rise. In 2009, an armed burka-clad man robbed a Scotiabank in Mississauga. On New Year's Eve 2010, a man in a burka committed a bank robbery in an Ottawa strip mall. Such incidents have occurred south of the border as well. An armed burka-clad man robbed a bank at gunpoint in North Carolina. A similar robbery took place in 2007 in Philadelphia, resulting in the death of a police man. Burka-clad criminals have committed similar robberies in the UK, where jewellery stores, sometimes owned by Muslims, have been robbed in the West Midlands, Glasgow and Oxfordshire. Similar crimes have taken place in the Middle East, with the niqab as the preferred disguise. According to one report, fifty people in Jordan have committed 170 crimes using the burka or niqab in a two-year period.

I must offer a word of clarification here. While I have argued that the burka can be an effective disguise, I have also repeatedly stressed that I never presented this evidence to implicate conservative Muslim women, or to suggest that they themselves were criminally involved. I provided the evidence merely to point out the burka's potential for being abused by criminals. This evidence helped me conclude that restricting the use of a garment that enables crime in this fashion would indeed be a reasonable curtailment of individual rights. It was constitutional as far as I was concerned. Governments have the right to legislate against any practice that is deemed detrimental to society. The above data about the burka and its misuse demonstrated beyond doubt that the garment can be a tool used by criminals. The burka was implicated in some of the most heinous crimes committed in Canada and abroad. This alone was enough grounds for banning the burka in public. However, there is further reason to restrict its use in public, which once again involves the issue of equality, peace and harmony in society.

I firmly believe that legislation protecting the rights of women who are forced into wearing the niqab is not only desirable but essential. The influence of radicalism grows stronger by the day. As more Muslims become radicalized, the expectation to wear the burka proliferates. This is so because burka advocates are stubbornly doctrinaire and their ultimate goal is to spread this practice among all Muslims by scaring them with hellfire theology. That is why I see an increasing number of burka-clad women in my neighbourhood mall. These swaddled women are barely able to contribute positively to society. They cannot easily become nurses or doctors, bus drivers or electricians. Indeed the impracticality of the burka marginalizes its wearers, and a society that allows such marginalization risks being perceived as dysfunctional. It seems burka advocates are concerned only about the rights of women to "choose" to wear a niqab or burka. The truth is that there are several other rights, of much greater importance, such as the right to choose what career to adopt and whom to marry, that these retrogressive advocates deliberately ignore.

Unveiled:

In Canada we must not allow the situation to get to the point Britain has reached on this issue. Because the burka has become so common in Britain, the government is reluctant to pass legislation against it. A similar scenario must be avoided in Canada and the United States, where the observance of the burka thankfully is not yet so widespread. Here the burka is still uncommon enough that courts can still debate whether to allow the testimony of veiled women. The Ontario Court of Appeal debated a test case of a Muslim sexual assault complainant in 2010, who insisted on remaining both invisible and anonymous, yet needed to testify in court. As expected, the woman's stance was supported by feminists, liberal activists and Muslim fundamentalists, all of whom cited her right to religious freedom. The Women's Legal Education and Action Fund (LEAF) was one such feminist group. Although it cautioned against using this case to set a precedent, the group made it clear that it wanted the court to accommodate the woman's request. I feared that would set the wrong precedent as Islamists would most certainly invoke it to advance their fundamentalist agenda.

This happened around the same time that Quebec also passed Bill 94, which would deny public services to women in veils. I sought an Islamist woman's opinion on Quebec Bill 94. She responded that, while religious *fatwa* (religious verdict) did not necessitate the niqab, religious *taqwa* (the desire to excel in faith) required that she don the face covering. With this in mind, she would abide by any laws requiring her to relinquish some of her religious freedoms, but insisted that such laws would interfere with her desire to excel in piety and religious observance. According to this woman, therefore, the niqab was clearly a religious preference rather than a requirement.

In April 2011 I was invited by the University of British Columbia to deliver their annual multiculturalism lecture, where I argued that the burka represented one extreme while nudity represented another. Both should be proscribed. Section 174 of the Criminal Code of Canada prohibits nudity in public places. People who wish to walk around nude in public places, including public offices, hospitals and schools, could object to such laws by citing the individual freedoms argument that burka adherents generally cite. They could very well state that their individual freedom to appear naked in public was curtailed. But were their rights absolute? Here we have two extreme situations. One of them entails a complete absence of clothing, while the other hides someone totally from view. If prohibiting the one extreme can be deemed constitutional in the interest of public welfare, then surely its opposite can also be, especially when it has the added disqualification of being a tool in the hands of criminals and terrorists.

At the lecture I delivered at the University of British Columbia, a member of the audience expressed concern that Muslim women would simply withdraw from society if they were forced to remove their veils in public. I responded that such a fear is too pessimistic. Such a conclusion is based on the flawed assumption that niqabi women will refuse to adhere to the law. Even the sexual assault complainant, known as N.S., has agreed to testify without her veil if she loses.

The issue of the burka ban in public would have to be assessed as a matter of common good rather than as a matter concerning the individual rights of a few women, some of whom I knew would be coerced into wearing such attire. I met a few university students at UBC who divulged to me that they were indeed being coerced. Moreover, religious freedoms could not be taken as an absolute. Restricting certain individual rights to advance the common good is not anti-democratic. People often assert that the right to choose what to wear is a democratic right. Indeed it is. However, democracy must not be confused with anarchy. Democratic societies must still regulate social interaction in public, and practices deemed detrimental to society must be subject to regulation. Canada has already done so in the case of public nudity. It must do so in the case of the burka as well, which constitutes the other extreme.

Based on the above arguments, I was able to convince many that a burka ban could easily be deemed constitutional. *Huffington Post Canada* asked me to engage in a public debate with Farah Mawani, a local activist, on who could change the most minds about the burka ban issue. I offered a discourse in the Huffington Post based on the above rationale and won the Huffington Post debate.

The argument from multiculturalism also needs to be addressed, as there are many who defend the burka from this perspective. They assert that different cultures have to be accepted on their own terms. If a culture considers the burka or hijab appropriate or even beneficial (and some Muslim women certainly regard it as beneficial) then this viewpoint must be accepted. Dr. Kathy Bullock, an Australian convert to Islam and an active member of the fundamentalist Islamic Society of North America (ISNA-Canada) devotes pages and pages of her book *Rethinking Muslim Women and the Veil* to proving just how wrong the West is in its perception of the veil as an oppressive garment. Because Muslim fundamentalism celebrates the burka and the resultant seclusion of women, an elaborate rationale exists to justify these practices. From this angle Kathy Bullock writes: "I argue that because of capitalism's emphasis on the body and materiality, wearing the hijab can be an empowering and liberating experience for women."[3]

Unveiled:

In my opinion, such discourse amounts to justifying the unjustifiable. Minorities within the diverse cultures of Canada that rationalize the subjugation of women in this fashion are not equal to cultures that don't. To assert this is not to discredit multiculturalism, which, correctly observed, is a noble concept. However, we must never tolerate the abuse of multiculturalism, and the type of political correctness that turns a blind eye to misogyny is just that sort of abuse.

Women who wear the face veil are in fact denied a face, a name and an identity. As a result of political correctness and narratives advanced by ultra-orthodox Muslims, many young Muslim women have been led to believe that in order to be respected they must assume the anonymity of the niqab or hijab. Such women include Cair-Can's Maryam Dadabhoy, whom I have debated on television. This sentiment is unfortunate. Muslim women must be respected simply because it is their human right to be respected–for who they are. What the conservatives fail to realize is that the minute they have decided to wear the niqab, they have acknowledged that they are not people but sex objects who need to be hidden from public gaze or else they will most certainly end up tempting men. They have allowed men to define them. Part of this sanctimonious narrative is the preposterous suggestion that the burka liberates women, and that women who wear it can engage fully in everyday life. Yet I have observed the difficulty with which burka-clad women eat in pubic, lifting their veil with one hand while trying to eat with the other. This is all quite unnecessary, as Islam does not even prescribe the face veil.

With that in mind, we must step beyond the choices of a small minority and consider the rights of society in general. We have seen how individual freedoms in a pluralistic society cannot be an absolute. The right of an individual to appear naked in public is not absolute. Why? Because in democratic societies, individual rights must be subordinated to collective rights, especially if the two come into conflict. And we most certainly have a conflict. Some women are being coerced into wearing the face veil. We must consider their rights. Citizens who do not cover their faces have the right to know who they are interacting with. What about their rights? The face veil is an insult to those who do not conceal their identity in public. In effect it says: "I have the right to know who you are but you don't have the right to know who I am."

Let us also look at the truth about the "choices" of Muslim women. Leila Hessini is a well-known scholar of women's rights in Islam: She believes that women who choose to wear the hijab and niqab are actually endorsing patriarchy rather than making a feminist choice. She states that these choices are made within the strictures of patriarchy. Their response is conditioned by the norms established by patriarchal cultures.

There are other reasons to consider the so-called choices of women to be not entirely genuine. Even Dr. Bullock, who defends the veil in her book *Rethinking Muslim Women and the Veil,* writes: "the relationship between an individual's culture and his or her ability to choose is complex, for choice is always circumscribed by the range between what a culture considers acceptable or unacceptable."[4] I would claim that the hijab and the niqab come into that very narrow range. Veiling is prescribed for Muslim women by the most conservative and patriarchal forces on the margins of the Muslim community. Women merely succumb to pressure from this influential minority and do not necessarily make a well-considered choice for themselves. A choice can be so called only among other choices. Women who opt to wear the face veil have often been exposed to only one narrow viewpoint within Islam, the one based on preaching about fear of public rebuke and even of hellfire. I therefore believe these women are not making a genuine choice but merely responding to fear. Muslim women are under tremendous pressure to conform to a particular school of thought within Islam. It is all part of the current politicization of Islam, with the niqab and burka as its most obvious and pernicious symbols.

I strongly believe that if presented with alternatives, women would choose not to wear the face veil. If they are offered sound theological reasons–and there are sound theological reasons to believe Islam does not mandate the face veil–I am convinced these women would choose not to hide themselves away.

If God truly wanted women to cover their hair or face, He would not have had to mince words. His injunction would have simply read: "Muslim women, cover your hair and your faces." I have challenged several Muslims to show me one verse of the Quran that talks in such unequivocal terms about veiling. No one has answered this challenge.

Third Wave Feminism and the Burka

I strongly believe that third-wave feminists are wrong to support the burka in Canada. Third wave feminism is based on moral relativism: it accepts all versions of feminine identity on their own terms. It allows women of various cultures to define roles for themselves without imposing standards from outside. Women therefore do not have to compete with men, for example, to prove their worth or their status in society. If women choose to be homemakers and mothers, it is their right and privilege to make those choices for themselves. If women choose to dress a certain way, it is all part of their feminine identity. In principle this is a valid stand, as it apparently rejects male roles in defining what it means to be female. However, third-wave feminism has missed the point in an important sense when it comes to the issue of the burka, niqab and even hijab.

Unveiled:

The feminist support of the burka fails to recognize that the face veil, indeed any form of veiling, is one of the most pernicious manifestations of patriarchy. I have often posed this question to feminists: is it a feminist option to "choose" a practice that is so steeped in patriarchy? It is in fact an oxymoron for women to say they are exercising their feminist right to choose to wear the burka. Any belief that allows such de facto male dominance is a strange thing to call feminism.

Third wave feminists therefore support a woman's right to wear the burka. I publicly debated one such feminist at the University of Toronto In February 2012. Professor Brenda Cossman, professor of law at the University of Toronto, like other third-wave feminists, stated that women who wore the burka had clearly chosen this path of femininity for themselves, and they must be supported in it. If there were contradictions in this perception, then her kind of feminism would accept those contradictions. To take away a woman's right to choose her own attire would mean imposing someone else's standards and understanding of equality and freedom. My reply stressed that women who don the burka have defined their femininity based on interpretations by men. Women who choose roles that stem from patriarchy have in fact had their roles defined for them. In the case of Muslim women, they have most certainly taken their cues from all the most chauvinistic and patriarchal interpretations of scripture and submissively embraced them without question. That women must accept polygamy, that they must veil before men, that they must stay confined to their domestic roles, are all ideas that have been handed down to women by men. Third-wave feminism therefore has built its case against a burka ban on a naïve and disturbing fallacy.

In December 2011, Canadian Minister of Citizenship, Immigration, and Multiculturalism Jason Kenney announced that Muslim women would be required to unveil at citizenship ceremonies. This was to affirm openness and gender equality as core Canadian values. In January 2012, the Muslim Canadian Congress honoured and applauded him officially for this bold stand.

Minister Kenney's move has drawn much criticism both from conservative segments of the Muslim community and from left-leaning feminists, who believe that such a ban violates the fundamental religious rights of Muslim women. That is where the burka debate currently stands in Canada. The continued opposition by these groups shows that more certainly needs to be done.

A Decade Opposing Jihadism

I became president of Muslims Against Terrorism soon after 9/11. I had not given much thought to the objectives and agendas of various Muslim organizations at that point in my career as an activist. I had not considered which among these groups might qualify as genuinely moderate. Perhaps this was because I was not as familiar with ideological differences among Muslims at that time. Islam is more often than not presented as a monolith. The founder of Muslims Against Terrorism, Syed Soharwardy, belongs to a Sufi order of Islam. He had sometimes spoken against violence and extremism as an advocate of Sufism, which tends to be more tolerant of other faiths than orthodox, mainstream Islam. That was good enough for me at that time. I later realized that Soharwardy was an Islamist of a different breed. That awareness for me came at the time the Sharia debate erupted in Ontario in 2003.

Sufi Muslims, and moderate Muslims generally, assert that violence and terror deviate from Islamic principles of tolerance and humanity. Terror is most certainly not inherent to the faith, they argue. Moderate Muslims also believe that jihad is to be waged only at the behest of an Islamic government and that it is allowed only in self-defence.

According to the accepted narrative, only Islamic governments are to declare a jihad under provocation from a non-Muslim source; individual Muslims are strictly prohibited from doing so. Based on this information, Muslims all across North America were stating that Islam was a peaceful religion and that the first caliph of Islam, Abu Bakr, had in fact prohibited the killing of non-combatants, children and women in a defensive war. He had also forbidden the destruction of trees or livestock. Verse 2:190 of the Quran states: "Fight in the name of Allah against those who fight you, but begin not hostilities. Lo Allah does not love the aggressors."

Like other moderate Muslims, I started opposing violence in the same manner by quoting verses of the Quran such as the above. There it was as plain as day: Allah abhorred aggression. Jihad was actually righteous and moral because it would be a fight against oppression. I searched for other verses of the Quran to build my thesis that the extremists were in fact misinterpreting the message of the Quran. Only later would I realize why extremists draw their inspiration from certain Quranic verses.

Other Muslim activists were also busy trying to dispel the perception that Islam preached violence against the infidel. But after the tragic 9/11 attacks, the Western world had hoped for a clear and universal repudiation of militant jihad from throngs of moderate Muslims. No doubt Muslim organizations condemned the attacks, but not strongly enough. These condemnations were usually accompanied by statements hinting that Western imperialism may have provoked the outrages.

In my opinion, Muslim reaction to 9/11 and ensuing terrorist activity has been half-hearted. It has been marked by confusion, indifference and in some cases acquiescence or even collusion. There are many underlying reasons for this apathy or belligerence. Anti-Western sentiment prevents many from recognizing that the greatest threat to Muslim harmony and progress is indeed the spread of jihadism and its resultant terror. Blinded by an inveterate hatred of the West, many Muslims feel that the jihadists are right in their struggle against Western hegemony. This sentiment remains highest in countries where jihadism enjoys great currency. These countries include Pakistan, Afghanistan, Yemen and Somalia. Because of this ongoing resentment, too many Islamists condone jihadist assaults on the West, either tacitly or overtly. The jubilation on the streets in some Muslim countries following the 9/11 attacks provided evidence of this. The perception among Muslims that they have suffered exploitation, oppression and subjugation at the hands of the West is fairly widespread, and the 9/11 attacks were seen as a long overdue victory for the Islamic world and just recompense for the "wrongdoings" of the West.

The festering Middle East conflict–the "black hole" of geopolitics–also gives Muslims the impression that the West is inherently anti-Muslim and that it is waging a war against Islam in its support for the state of Israel. They also cite the Crusades as proof of the historic animosity between the Christian world and the Islamic world. Islamists therefore consider jihad imperative to regain their lost ascendancy and to preserve Islamic values, culture and civilization.

Thus jihadists and their apologists believe the political contexts warranting jihad have been recreated in our contemporary world and that Islam is somehow under attack today, as it was in its formative years. Seventh century Arabia saw the dawn of Islam amid great turmoil. The fledgling Muslim community in Mecca was under constant attack from the pagans, and Muslims had to fight for their very survival. Many contemporary jihadists claim to feel threatened in similar fashion. Muslims are also bound by the notion that sharia law is immutable and that the tenets of Islam are true for all times. This logic suggests that jihad too is timeless.

The Muslims I have debated on jihad also propose poverty and socioeconomic marginalization as possible reasons for jihadist anger. However, I have often pointed out that terrorists come from all walks of life. Many known terrorists are educated professionals, such as doctors and engineers.

I have hence decided that jihadism is ideologically based. After examining some jihadist literature, I am reasonably sure that the medieval Islamic concept of jihad and the contemporary terrorist agenda have become conflated in the minds of the jihadists. They equate jihad with terror mainly due to the Quran's retributive law of equivalence. It was a form of tribal justice demanding eye-for-an-eye revenge. Contemporary jihadists believe that this Quranic provision allows them to kill indiscriminately because, in their view, Muslim blood has also been shed indiscriminately in Western mass bombings.

In fact the jihadists have formulated an elaborate rationale to justify violence because of this conflation. That rationale is rather difficult to dislodge, as it is not reason but anger which drives it. It has forced me to look for theological answers to combat such notions as I believe Islamists can be persuaded to discard radicalism only through religious discourse. What follows are my conclusions on jihad and how to combat extremism.

Historians of the Quran agree that verse 2:190 (quoted earlier) was the first to enjoin jihad on the newly emerging community of believers. The verse urges Muslims to oppose any aggressors, but stresses that Allah has no sympathy for those who start hostilities. Those who argue in favour of "defensive" jihad often quote this verse.

Islamic history, however, appears to invalidate the above contention. The early Muslims had been recently displaced from Mecca, their home town. Upon arrival in Medina, they were paired with the local residents for support and help, but the local "Ansars" or helpers were reluctant to extend their help indefinitely. And although they agreed to embrace the new faith and protect its foreign adherents, the Muhajirun (those who migrated) would still need a source of income to survive in the new city. The Meccan Muslims were also alone in their fight against pagan military onslaughts. According to Mohammad Marmaduke Pickthall, the helpers' oath of allegiance "had not included fighting in the field."[1] That the Medinans were exempt from fighting is further indication that the Meccan Muslims' initial armed struggle was largely to recover their lost goods and possessions. It was these economic realities that would occasion jihad—sometimes pre-emptive. That indeed was the justification provided in the Quran for warfare, as the Meccans had been driven out from their homes. The Quran states:

"And kill them wherever you find them and drive them out from where they drove you out, for persecution is worse than killing. And fight them not in and near the sacred mosque, but if they fight you, then fight them. Such is the requital for disbelievers. But if they desist then surely Allah is most forgiving, merciful. And fight them until there is no persecution and religion is freely professed for Allah. But if they desist then remember that no hostility is allowed except against the aggressor. (Quran 2: 192—194)

Indeed one often hears that Islam permits jihad only in self-defence. People are then puzzled when they see unprovoked terrorist attacks. How does one resolve this apparent contradiction? The Quranic commentator Mohammad Asad affirms the defensive nature of jihad when he states: "This and the following verse lay down unequivocally that only self-defence, in the widest sense of the word, makes war permissible for Muslims....This early fundamental principle of self-defence as the only possible justification of war has been maintained throughout the Quran"[2].

Yet Asad's words are telling. In my opinion, the "widest sense" means that wars of aggression can be construed by jihadists as defensive. They may very well consider such "retaliation" just recompense for all the wrongs done to Muslims. These admonitions are repeated in verse 40 of Chapter 8 in the Quran: "And fight them until there is no persecution and religion is wholly for Allah. But if they desist, then surely Allah is watchful of what they do." (Quran 8:40).

What comprises persecution is open to interpretation, so that jihadists can attach any meaning to it that suits their agenda. Alleged persecution can thus condone vicious pre-emptive strikes by jihadists, especially when they invoke the Quran's retributive law of equality. Mohammad Marmaduke Pickthall also agrees that "the Prophet had always intended to attack the caravan." [3]. This was the caravan headed to Syria under the auspices of Abu Sufyan, the leader of the Meccan pagans, who later converted to Islam. The verse quoted below adds to this perspective on jihad. The verse reads:

"The violation of the sacred month should be retaliated in the sacred month. And for all sacred things there is the law of retaliation. So whoso punishes you, punish him for his transgression to the extent to which he has transgressed against you. And fear Allah and know that Allah is with those who fear him." (Quran 2:195)

This verse, when read in conjunction with verse 2: 192, opens the door to pre-emptive wars based on jihadist perceptions of persecution and wrongdoing, "for persecution is worse than killing". The above verse states that the retribution must be proportional, not more and not less. But all a jihadist needs to believe is that wrong has been done; jihad must then be undertaken to rectify it.

In June 2006 the story broke of the eighteen Toronto-based terror suspects. These were young men plotting to kill the Prime Minister and blow up the CN Tower. Six years after their arrest, questions still remain as to why some Canadians of Muslim origin would wish their fellow citizens such harm. The Quranic interpretations discussed above may explain this belligerence. The arrest of three more Canadian Muslim men in Ottawa in 2009 for alleged links to Al Qaeda demands that we again examine the real causes of jihadism and its unfortunate link with terror.

The world is familiar with the Danish Jyllands-Posten cartoon controversy. One caricature of the prophet in particular greatly inflamed Muslim sentiment. I came across several Muslims at the time who thought that such a cartoon showed that the West was insensitive to Islam. They argued that this must be deliberate, as the West has always harboured antipathy toward Islam and its adherents, and the depiction of the prophet as a terrorist was simply one instance of that inveterate hatred. They crowded the streets demanding death for infidels, burning vehicles and smashing windows. Portraying the founder of the Islamic faith as a terrorist implied that all those who follow him are also terrorists.

The outrage continued for months. Here in Canada, newspapers and journals decided not to reprint the controversial cartoons. Ezra Levant, then publisher of the magazine *Western Standard*, was the lone exception. It landed him in a lawsuit with the founder of the Islamic Supreme Council of Canada, Imam Syed Soharwardy, who had been my former colleague in fighting jihadism.

Soharwardy withdrew that lawsuit but insisted that Islam does not permit violence except in self-defence. I was puzzled. Whose understanding of jihad was right: the terrorists who believe wanton killing is permitted or the Sufis who preach a less aggressive message? I opened my Quran once more to look for answers. What struck me was the distinction between the Islam of Mecca and the Islam of Medina. Meccan Islam was preoccupied with belief and hardly ever mentioned jihad. Medinan Islam, which came later, shifted focus from belief to conquest and war, and introduced the idea of jihad in stages, ultimately giving full authority to the prophet Mohammad to subjugate non-believers.

Unveiled:

It was during the Medinan period that the pagans were barred from entering Mecca and Medina. It was also during the Medinan period that Allah declared Islam to be the only acceptable religion. From then on, jihad was to be fought aggressively.

Moderate Muslims insist that verses of the Quran are read out of context by jihadi terrorists. However, they should take the matter beyond this mere acknowledgement. The time has long passed for such verses to be placed in the context of a bygone era. Moderate Muslims must urgently challenge violent interpretations based on ancient events. My aunt, Dr. Riffat Hassan, also believes that the radical clerics must be convinced through better religious argument.

The theological base of violent jihad must be shown as invalid for modern times by arguing that the cultural and political landscape of seventh century Arabia was completely different from that of today. Jihadists must understand that social, historical and political contexts can never be recreated in full. No two contexts are identical. Therefore no doctrine, including the doctrine of jihad, can be transferred intact from one place and time to another.

The context of jihad in the seventh century was the establishment of a new monotheistic faith amid pagan idolatry and economic warfare. The pagans of Mecca tolerated competing religious views. Jews, Christians, Hanifs, Sabians and others simply went about practicing their faiths while the idolaters continued their centuries-old traditions. What was it then about Islam's message that pitted various religious communities against each other?

Arabia of the seventh century was perpetually locked in tribal warfare. Each indigenous Arabian clan worshipped a different god or totem. Wells were to be defended in that desert landscape, where water was a scarce resource. Thus religion was a tribal matter. No clan challenged the beliefs of another clan as long as their lives and property were protected. The different gods of the various tribes were housed in the Kaaba in Mecca. Here any tribal warfare would have to be forgotten to facilitate trading. The precincts of the Kaaba and Mecca would have to be considered a safe haven, something that Islam was to uphold. No fighting or warfare was permitted near Mecca, especially in the four sacred months of the year.

In my opinion, polytheistic religions are generally more tolerant of other beliefs than monotheistic faiths. Amid this atmosphere of religious tolerance within the precincts of Mecca, a new faith, even a monotheistic one, need not have disrupted the status quo. However, the prophet Mohammad was adamant about spreading his message beyond tribal boundaries. As a man preoccupied with the transcendent and given to reflection and meditation, he was convinced of the truth of his monotheistic message. His desire to transcend the boundaries of tribal affiliation would disrupt the existing social order. No longer tenable was the open-minded notion of "to each his own." This was a man from the Qureish clan who was rebelling against ancient beliefs, but he was also gathering support for his views from outside sources. He reached out to black and white, rich and poor, man and woman alike. His message was one of equality and social justice and he began to gain many supporters. Symbolically his monotheistic message meant that all tribal gods were false, and that the God of Islam–Allah–was the God of all peoples. This monotheistic message had the makings of a universal message that would eliminate tribal, class and (to an extent) gender inequalities and differences. This one God spoke to all his people through the mouth of the prophet himself, in powerful verses that later came to be known as the Quran.

Some heeded the message but others opposed it. This opposition was couched in religious terms, but Mohammad's preaching was in fact an implicit challenge to all the existing institutions of the society. It called into question the worship of tribal gods, the economic life attached to their shrines, the values of tribal tradition, the authority of the chiefs and the solidarity of the clans from which Mohammad wished to draw his followers. Religion, moral belief, social structure, and economic life formed a system of ideas and institutions inextricably bound up with one another. To attack them at any major point was to attack the whole society, root and branch. The revelations of the Quran provided Mohammad with a response to his opponents. His preaching was justified because he was sent by God to rescue his people from ignorance and guide them on the path to righteousness. He was a prophet in the long succession from the Old and New Testaments, and furthermore he was sent to declare God's will in Arabic. At this stage Mohammad included Christians and Jews, as well as pagans, in his mission. Only later did it become clear that his preaching would establish a new religion alongside Judaism and Christianity.

Mohammad's Islam therefore was very different from the prevalent religions of the time. His religion sought to disrupt the status quo, not only by supplanting other faiths with Islam, but also by disrupting the economic lifeline of the Arabian peninsula, destroying existing family structures, and by creating rifts between family members on the one hand and uniting them under the banner of Islam on the other. In short, a new community and tribe would emerge on the basis of faith, one that would in a few short years dominate all of Hejaz (the western part of Arabia) and within a century spread across three continents, taking in its grip the Iberian peninsula as well.

The opposition to Mohammad's message in Mecca therefore was manifold. Clans objected because many of their sons and daughters were leaving the old religion to embrace the prophet's monotheistic creed. The socially marginalized were also some of the earlier converts to Islam as they were attracted to the prophet's social justice message. Abyssinian slaves, women and the impoverished readily heeded his call. Such converts were hardly likely to provide the kind of army that would lead Islam into its dazzling future of victory and conquest. Such an army would begin to materialize in Medina.

The pagan Qureish, who already worshipped Allah along with other deities, were upset with Mohammad's admonitions about hellfire. They were not accustomed to belief in a hereafter where their bodies would be resurrected and subjected to torment if they refused to believe correctly. Shunning other gods beside Allah created particular resistance among the Qureish of Mecca, who were also disaffected because Mohammad's new tribe of believers would challenge their economic dominance in the region. These were the circumstances that would eventually necessitate jihad. Hostilities continued and jihad was conceived, but only after the prophet had migrated with his band of a few hundred followers to Medina.

Islamists' contemporary agenda is similar to that of the early Muslims, which is to replace Islam with all other religions. However, the social, political and economic contexts are vastly different from what they were in the seventh century.

Mecca's ancient pluralistic tradition was disrupted, with grave consequences for the peace and stability of Hejaz. Today Islamists threaten the peace and stability of the world, showing the same religious zeal as the early Muslims. But the aim of the early warriors of Islam was not entirely religious. It was as much economic as it was political. According to John Esposito, "Mecca and Medina became locked in an intense struggle to win over other towns and groups of nomads, a struggle in which Mecca, with its established commercial and tribal ties, initially appeared to have the advantage. Mohammad, however, launched raids against the Meccan caravans, seizing valuable booty and hostages, and more important, disrupting the commercial lifeblood of Mecca." [4]

Also according to Esposito, the objective of these raids or *ghazwaat*, as they were called in Arabic, was commercial, political and at times territorial. Because the results of the battles were somewhat inconclusive in the beginning, the warring parties were also forced to enter into a truce from time to time. This truce led to the annual Hajj pilgrimage being permitted to the Muslims, eventually placing them in a better bargaining position against the Meccan Qureish.

It is useful to look at the sources of livelihood available to Muslims in that nascent religious community. While Muslim historians have traditionally depicted the conflicts between the Meccans and the Muslims as a struggle between good and evil, with the Muslims naturally being on the side of the righteous and oppressed, it is well documented both within Muslim and non-Muslim historical sources that the early Muslims resorted to warfare and conquest to survive as an emerging community. This course of action was considered justifiable by both the early Muslims and contemporary believers, as the early Muslims had purportedly been driven out of their homes by the infidels.

The Meccan Qureish had felt threatened by the Muslim presence in Medina, as their trade route to Syria passed through Muslim territory, and they had even warned the Medinans not to side with the Muslims. As skirmishes between the Meccans and the Muslims had already occurred in the two years before the Battle of Badr, the Muslims thought it necessary to strengthen their hold over the trade route. The Qureish caravan returning from Syria was carrying great wealth in the form of gold coins. The prophet felt justified in attacking the caravan in order to recover the wealth that had purportedly been lost to Muslims upon their exit from Mecca. He allowed the raids in order to relieve the growing poverty among the Muslim immigrants of Medina. This poverty had caused serious dissension among them and the profession of faith in God as unity was in itself under serious threat. These wars therefore may have occurred from a combination of religious motives and the desire for steady income.

The Quran speaks clearly about the distribution of war booty. One fifth of it was to go to Allah and his messenger, and the rest was to be divided among the Muslim warriors, the mendicants and the handicapped. Income was generated not only by the booty collected, but also by demanding ransom for captives. Many of the elite from the prophet's army, including Omar, the future caliph of Islam, had suggested putting the captives to death. However, it was decided that ransom would be more beneficial for the long term interests of the community. Abu Bakr is reported to have said that the captives were all relatives of the Muslims. Ransoming them would also greatly strengthen the economic power of Muslims and give them victory over the unbelievers. Even according to renowned Muslim scholars like Ameer Ali, "War between the Qureish and the Muslims lay in the logic of the commercial geography of North Arabia." [5]

Perhaps the circumstances around the subsequent Battle of the Trench can shed further light on the motives behind the earlier manifestations of jihad. Some of the causes were indeed economic, as evidenced by other accounts. In 627 AD, a confederate army consisting of Jews and Arab pagans surrounded Medina, where the prophet's three thousand or so followers were based. The confederate army consisted of about ten thousand warriors and six hundred camels. The siege lasted a couple of weeks, after which the supplies of the confederates began to dwindle. The prophet and his companions, realizing that they were greatly outnumbered, dug a trench around Medina at the behest of one Salman Farsi. The trench was wide enough to prevent the camels and horses from jumping over it.

As the siege was unsuccessful, it dealt a severe blow to Meccan trade. The Meccans were crushed economically and the Muslims under the leadership of their prophet emerged as the most influential power in the region. Nevertheless, great opposition to the mission of the prophet persisted. Meccan chief Abu Sufyan forged alliances with the Jews of Medina. It is unclear whether this was for doctrinal reasons alone, or whether there was more to it, such as economic warfare. Even some nomadic tribes joined the confederate forces in their resistance to the prophet Mohammad.

Doubtless, that context of economic warfare contained discernible religious overtones. It was an era when religion was dominant in the lives of people. Religious identities were strong, but assuming that the motives of these wars were exclusively religious may be wrong on several counts. The Byzantine and Sassanian empires before the rise of Islam had also been engaged in warfare for political, territorial and economic control. With the rise of Islam, there was a third force in the region to contend with, one which had a different cultural and religious identity from the Byzantines and the Sassanians but was nonetheless seeking hegemony in the region. According to John Esposito, this expansionism was no doubt motivated by religious zeal, but also by economic factors. Even the warring tribes of Arabia, who had come within the fold of Islam during the prophet's lifetime, rebelled because they refused to pay the *zakat* tax levied on Muslims. As for other non-Muslim peoples brought under Islam's domination, the citizens were in fact left free to practice their faith by paying the *dhimmi* tax imposed on them. There was definitely an economic benefit to be gained by keeping the non-Muslim population outside Islam's fold–a further indication that the ultimate objective of the *ghazwat* was not always to spread Allah's message. Had the intent been to convert all to Islam, the economic benefits would have been greatly compromised. Esposito writes:

"Mecca and Medina became locked in an intense struggle to win over other towns and groups of nomads, a struggle in which Mecca, with its established commercial and tribal ties, initially appeared to have the advantage. Mohammad however launched raids against the Meccan caravans, seizing valuable booty and hostages, and more important disrupting the lifeblood of Mecca."[6]

Modern jihadists, on the other hand, are expansionist primarily to ensure the supremacy of Islam for religious reasons. But such religious imperialism has no place in our modern world, where nations prefer to resolve their disputes through negotiation and compromise; where modern warfare, if it must be undertaken, is governed strictly by the Geneva Conventions; where human rights have been enshrined in the UN Declaration of Human Rights; where slavery and the subjugation of women have been declared morally reprehensible.

Jihad is an obsolete concept. The concept of war in Islam came about because Islam was a new religion and struggled to survive in a hostile environment. The early Muslims resorted to warfare and conquest to survive as an emerging religious and political community, but the circumstances no longer exist to warrant such moves.

Proving a concept obsolete is a painfully difficult task within Islam's theological framework, as traditional Muslims assert that Quranic injunctions are timeless and immutable. They insist that the Quran's retributive law of equality warrants jihad, as Muslims are only avenging "Western domination". The Quranic law of equality legitimizes revenge equal to injury. Therefore if Muslim children are killed by enemy bombs, it is justified to kill enemy children. This is how jihadists conflate jihad with terror. But this conflation is once again fallacious.

For example, the retributive law of equality operates only in a tribal setting. Every tribe in Arabia subscribed to that form of justice. The justice system today has undergone a drastic change from those days of eye-for an-eye retribution. A tribal system of justice is obviously outmoded compared to modern, enlightened means for citizens or nations to seek redress for wrongdoings. International courts of justice are now available for communities who consider their religious, ethnic or national rights violated.

Furthermore, when the jihadists invoke a blanket eye-for-an-eye retributive law to the letter, they are also violating the spirit of the Quran's retributive law of equality. The Quran states the following about who bears the burden of sins:

"He who follows the right way follows it only for the good of his own soul; and he who goes astray, goes astray only to his own loss. And no bearer of burden shall bear the burden of another. And we shall never punish until we have sent a Messenger. (Quran 17:13-15)

Another verse states:
"That no bearer of burden shall bear the burden of another, And that man will have nothing but what he strives for; And that the result of his striving shall soon be known; Then will he be rewarded for it with the fullest reward; And that with thy Lord is the final judgment; (Quran 53:38-42)

If one were to interpret the above verses literally, it would become apparent that the terrorists are entirely wrong in attacking innocent civilians based on a strictly theological standpoint. Killing innocent people violates an important Islamic theological principle: that no soul shall bear the burden of another. One person cannot be punished for the sins of another. Terrorism manifestly violates this principle, as it kills indiscriminately. Equal revenge, as embodied in the Quran's law of equality, cannot possibly be implemented in the contemporary world.

Who, for example, is able to determine what equal retribution is? Can one guarantee that injury inflicted on the enemy is strictly commensurate with the collective injury supposedly suffered by Muslims? Perhaps the example from Portia in *The Merchant of Venice* can be used to illustrate this point. Shylock demanded a pound of Antonio's flesh if the latter defaulted in his payment of Shylock's debt on time. But Shylock did not clarify that blood ought not be spilled. That was not part of the loan contract. What yardstick do terrorists have to ensure that proportional justice has been meted out to enemies? Can they keep a count of civilians killed in a terrorist attack? What if the enemy has killed only four Muslims and five of the enemy civilians get killed? How is that absolutely equal retribution? No such action can be considered proportional within the framework of the retributive law of equality. It is an untenable concept.

The terrorists are perhaps led astray by Quranic verses that appear to contradict the above notion, such as the following:

"O ye who believe! respond to Allah, and the Messenger when he calls you that he may give you life, and know that Allah comes in between a man and his heart, and that He it is unto Whom you will be gathered. And beware of an affliction which will surely not smite exclusively those among you who have done wrong. And know that Allah is severe in requiting. (Quran 8:24-25)

How is one to resolve the discrepancy then? Certainly, the natural disasters spoken of in the Quran seem to engulf the good and the bad. When the Quran states that no soul shall bear the burden of another, is it referring only to the judgment reserved for the afterlife? Moreover, how does the Quran's retributive law of equality come to bear on this apparent contradiction? Does it support the contradiction or does it negate it?

Jihadists believe that the later Medinan verses enjoining jihad supersede the Meccan verses which advocate peace and forgiveness. However, this is not universally accepted by Muslims, who insist that the Quran must be read in totality. According to this moderate view, the verses on peace and forgiveness are just as relevant as the militant verses. The more universal message of these verses must be chosen above the belligerent injunctions, which relate only to a specific ancient context.

Certainly, the more humane notion of the Quran that no soul shall bear the burden of another should be upheld to resolve any contradiction. This principle was once before observed by the prophet's army when a general amnesty was declared on pagans after the conquest of Mecca. Modern jihadists must look to their own past when interpreting verses of the Quran on jihad.

The modern conflation of jihad and terror violates the very principles upon which the jihadists themselves draw, and is therefore ideologically flawed. The retributive law of equality would also demand that the Geneva Conventions of armed conflict be duly acknowledged and observed. According to the Conventions, civilians must not be harmed. Western countries strive to abide by these regulations, and although civilian deaths do occur, Western policy is to avoid non-combatant casualties. When terrorists attack civilians, they are in fact violating their own retributive law of equality, as their civilians have not been intentionally attacked by those who abide by the Geneva Conventions, whereas the terrorists intentionally slaughter civilians.

For countries that abide by the Geneva Conventions, the intentional killing of civilians is strictly prohibited. It is true that in any combat, civilian casualties can always occur. However, an apology always follows such blunders. Terrorists, on the other hand, make no apologies for civilian casualties. The jihadists are in gross violation of the retributive law of equality, as the inequality lies in the difference in intent.

The conflation of jihad and terror thus occurs mainly because of a misapplication of the Quran's retributive law. It is on this flawed basis that jihadists condone the killings of innocent civilians. The difference in intent signals a crucial difference between the violence perpetrated by jihadists and Western standards of warfare. If the retributive law of equality is to be used, the jihadists are not entitled to cherry-pick parts of it that suit their gruesome agenda.

Modern jihadists, possibly not aware of the historical causes of jihad, have mostly chosen a strictly theological agenda. Yet the early causes of jihad were more economic and political than theological. The contexts that occasioned them no longer exist. That was an era where conquest and colonialism were accepted. Islam carried out its own conquests as part of that great colonial surge. The reasons were mostly economic and political, even though the entity that acted as the great colonial power of those times was defined in religious terms. Conquest and domination proved a useful source of income for that nascent Islamic community, but it can no longer be tolerated. The United Nations as an international watchdog has the authority to pass resolutions against nations who violate the sovereignty of other nations. Jihad is a medieval concept that has no place in our contemporary world.

Addressing the Muslim Anti-Western Narrative

I have often attempted to dispel the seething anti-Western narrative that turns some Muslim youth into radicals, but it has become as ingrained as a new kind of religion. The most extreme of the anti-US flag-burners–those who see 9/11 as a Bush or Mossad conspiracy–have beliefs that are so outrageous that they are beyond redemption. But hopefully the opinions in this chapter will help in some way to make another side more credible at least to those with views that are a little more moderate.

Muslims across the world are convinced that the West always acts against their interests. Whether it is the West supporting the state of Israel, craving Middle East oil, deposing or installing puppet regimes, or siding with what are deemed "anti-Islam" forces, most Muslims remain suspicious and distrustful of the West. In recent times, particularly in the aftermath of 9/11, this perception has caused special resentment. Muslims living in the West also see their faith, practices and culture constantly under scrutiny, which further sharpens their hostility toward the West. Many insist there is a Western conspiracy against Islam. Some Muslims even secretly believe that Westerners and non-Muslims know Islam is the truth and oppose it for that very reason!

The continued support of Israel by the West puts it at loggerheads with Islam. Most Muslims identify with Palestinians. They also feel a sense of religious entitlement to the city of Jerusalem, from where the prophet Mohammad is said to have mounted a winged horse to travel through the heavens for a meeting with the Almighty. They resent it that almost seven decades after of the birth of the state of Israel, the Palestinians remain disenfranchised.

Political conflicts across the world also intensify this resentment. In recent times, the wars in Afghanistan and Iraq and the so-called war on terror have further solidified this Muslim antipathy in the world towards the West. Muslims see civilian deaths, the drone attacks in Pakistan and Bush's "shock and awe" as blatant Western aggression against Muslims and a way to usurp their resources.

Elsewhere, the West is seen as meddling in Muslim affairs by installing dictators who will kowtow to its demands. Turning a blind eye to the Saudi monarchy, propping up Hosni Mubarak in Egypt and installing Hamid Karzai in Afghanistan, all appear hypocritical to Muslims. From the Shah of Iran's opulence and oppression to the overthrow of Saddam in Iraq, the Muslim world sees the decadent and imperialistic West as rapacious and meddlesome. Muslims believe the US policy in the Middle East is only about seizing oil resources. Misinformation drives much of this sentiment. It is about time some myths were exposed.

America has always been an easy scapegoat. If American soldiers go into Muslim countries, anti-American hordes begin to claim that Uncle Sam's commercial interests pull all the strings behind the scenes. America is seen as the bully with the big bucks. In a globalised world, US companies are inevitably prominent. America (and the Jews) are therefore held responsible for all the ills in the Muslim world. Muslims who deny this are often told they are ignorant and don't look into issues deeply enough.

The required depth has a lot to do with media. The standard Muslim narrative on these issues is bolstered by set ideas about reliable sources of news and commentary. Al Jazeera may be considered acceptable, but other mainstream news sources such as CNN and the BBC are seen as superficial and biased, though what they report is happily treated as factual if it fits the narrative, such as a tragically misguided missile hitting an Afghan village. Fringe bloggers and columnists with the "correct" political credentials are praised, as are anti-US writers such as Noam Chomsky and Robert Fisk. For those who never read books, Michael Moore's *Fahrenheit 911* will do as part of the defining gospel. It helps if the purveyors of the narrative can claim that the forces of the establishment do everything they can to suppress the truth which these noble and selfless campaigners are trying to reveal. Oddly, these campaigners seem to have no difficulty getting their books published and documentaries distributed.

It can be useful to seize upon a little-known aspect of a conflict which, if massaged the right way, reflects very badly on Western (usually US) policy. An example of this was the claim that the US was really in Afghanistan to clear the way for a pipeline as a safe conduit for oil and gas extracted from Central Asian republics. While it is true that US interests did investigate this possibility, it never became serious policy, and a route through Azerbaijan and Georgia was preferred. However, most people of course know nothing about any of this, and little interest in nosing out the truth.

Those who push the anti-US agenda can easily draw attention to this angle on US policy and crank it up as a motive. The advocate, possessing information that listeners or readers do not, can easily appear knowledgeable and gain the upper hand in presenting an argument. When the "fact" is very obscure, the suggestion can easily be made that it has been suppressed by the puppeteers who control the mainstream media. All this strengthens the anti-Western narrative.

What further reinforces the narrative is America's "damned if it does and damned if it doesn't" dilemma in international affairs. Any action or inaction simply reinforces the dogma. The same people fault the US equally for what it did in Iraq and is not doing in Syria. Those who revile it as the world's policeman for intervention can be the first to criticize it for sitting on its hands when it shows restraint. No action it takes (or declines to take) can ever free it from condemnation.

The case of Afghanistan shows this most poignantly. When the Americans invaded the country just after 9/11, their actions had considerable support, even from the political left. Sympathy for the Americans after the outrages in Washington, New York and Shanksville was still strong enough to win over all but its most ferocious critics. However, the condition often added was that the Americans must not simply hit and run; they must not abandon Afghanistan as they did after the Soviets left. The US had supplied the Afghan holy warriors with arms to fight the Russians, but simply abandoned the country after that. In fairness to the oppressed Afghan people, it could not forsake that benighted country again after its goal of routing the Taleban and al Qaeda was achieved.

A fair condition. Yet that leads to a conundrum. Taking no action would be considered abandonment, but what would appropriate support be, and in what form could it be delivered? The US could not simply hand over billions of dollars with no strings attached, because the money would just disappear, snatched by corrupt regional warlords in that fractured country. If it sent well-funded experts, such as soil scientists, doctors and engineers, to help the country develop, they would not be safe in a lawless land with a sizable minority of barbarians who would happily abduct infidels or even behead them with barely a moment's hesitation. Therefore, in order to make the place safe for development, it needed to station soldiers there in order to establish enough security for a measure of progress to occur. Hence the militarization. Which imperfect choice made more sense ethically, economically or politically: on the one hand, abandonment; on the other, intervention with military backup? Either one admirably serves the anti-American narrative.

Those millions of Muslims who accept the anti-US narrative see the Western presence there as imperialistic. The most hateful among them use Afghanistan as a means of recruiting jihadists, and rhetorically ask impressionable young Islamist men if they can tolerate seeing the deaths of so many innocent Muslim children without taking up arms–or building bombs full of nails–against the invaders. Yet the vast numbers of people whom American and Nato forces would ideally like to help in Afghanistan are themselves Muslims. Of course, it would be impossible for those Muslims who hate the US to concede that its intervention in a Muslim country can ever seek to benefit local people.

Interventions in Iraq and Afghanistan were indeed partly about power. Islamists get furious when they consider the projection of Western military and economic power. However, they take for granted powerful vested interests in the Muslim world which they seek to preserve. Their ideal Islamic society is a medieval one in which extraordinary despotic power is wielded by men (always men) in privileged positions in government and in families. Western infidel forces would import the kind of universal human rights which would threaten this cozy setup.

No nation which is big and influential enough to play an international role can claim a spotless record on the world stage (the Arabs themselves have been expansionist). The US has supported some brutal dictators in the past, but much less so in recent years. In fact, the much maligned Bush/Cheney philosophy vehemently opposed puppet regimes. The majority of Muslims contend that the US-led war on Iraq was waged simply for the US to gain access to Iraqi oil. It was a war motivated by greed, it resulted in the massive killings of Iraqi civilians and the West was to blame. Yet the invasion, unsuccessful though it turned out to be, was the very antithesis of puppetry. If the US had sought cheap oil and a compliant despot at any human cost, it would have made no sense to invade Iraq; it would have been much easier to whisper to Saddam that they would keep quiet about the Iraqis who disappear in the night, and just invite him to sign oil contracts. Such a policy would be the easiest and cheapest way to keep the oil flowing and the downtrodden suppressed.

Moreover, before the invasion, the Americans worked hard at diplomatic negotiations to gather support from other countries to topple Saddam, as had happened successfully in the first Gulf War. This was not the action of an administration that unilaterally sought to plunder a helpless nation. Oil was admittedly part of the US motive. However, it sought to make it available, rather than steal it. Events after the war confirm this. The Iraqi government has put contracts for developing oil fields up for open tender, with successful bids from a huge variety of oil companies so far. Some companies from Western coalition countries have won contracts, but so have companies from non-combatant nations, including China, Malaysia, Korea and Norway. The Bush administration, for all its naïve blundering in Iraq, at least helped to install an Iraqi government which is sufficiently independent to formulate policies which do not necessarily favour the US.

America has in fact helped Muslims many times in recent years, sometimes to its own detriment. It is useful to look behind the headlines and examine one such case in detail. After 9/11, the US agreed to pay Uzbekistan, a nation which is overwhelmingly Sunni Muslim, to use Karshi-Khanabad air base as a staging post for operations into Afghanistan. However, the Americans became concerned about repression by the autocratic President Karimov. In particular, around five hundred people are believed to have been killed in the Andijan massacre in 2005. Karimov had been using the threat of terrorism as a pretext to suppress all dissent.

The American administration pressured the Uzbek government to allow an international investigation and to allow safe passage for refugees who, according to diplomat R. Nicholas Burns, would have suffered persecution if they returned to Uzbekistan. The Uzbek regime found such US pressure intolerable, and the US military was duly expelled from Uzbekistan. Furthermore, the US call for democratization in Uzbekistan drove the disillusioned Karimov back into the Russian sphere of influence. He even asked the Russians to upgrade its relationship with Uzbekistan to a full-blown alliance. Thus it was that an American administration with a profound interest in operating a military base in a Muslim nation voluntarily gave it up in the interests of improving the rights of that nation's citizens. This is not the action of an imperialist state bent on hegemony or on repression of ordinary Muslims.

I constantly hear that Americans and Westerners kill Muslims mercilessly. They talk about carpet bombings in Afghanistan, "shock and awe" in Iraq and drone attacks in Pakistan. Each time some of us have denounced terror, we get a response from some angry Islamist or other asking "What about all the Muslims that are being killed as a result of Western aggression?" The perception of Americans among Muslims is that they want to rape their lands and strip them of their religious identity. I strongly believe that America's intentions are misunderstood. Muslims must examine the American record in defending human rights. It necessarily involves coming into conflict with religion, for example on issues concerning women. This does not mean that Westerners are anti-Muslim *per se;* it is just that the worst transgressions against human rights continue to occur in Muslim countries.

Civilian deaths in Iraq before the US invasion provided sheaths of misinformation and propaganda for the anti-US Muslim narrative. In the 1990s the US and Britain imposed two no-fly zones in Iraq to help protect the Shiite marsh Arabs in the south and the Kurds in the north, thousands of whom Saddam had eliminated. When allied planes flew patrols in these zones, Iraqi ground defences sometimes fired at them. The allied planes responded and destroyed the defence battery. These batteries were often deliberately located in populated areas, and Saddam wrung every propaganda advantage he could from the casualties.

Much was also made of the deaths of children from the effects of UN sanctions during the 1990s, for example from shortages of medicine and baby food. Early in the sanctions period, the Americans and British allowed Iraq to sell a measured amount of its oil legally, to provide medicine and necessities. Saddam used this money primarily to build more palaces. The sanctions policy was flawed in many ways, but it was a sincere attempt to make the best of a crisis made insurmountable not by cynical anti-Muslim Western policy but by the vanity and callousness of an Arab dictator.

A good case can be made to criticize US foreign policy throughout the twentieth century, and especially in the decades after World War Two. In Latin America it often supported brutal regimes, either openly or surreptitiously. The CIA's clandestine intervention poisoned local politics in ways that may not yet have been fully revealed. However, this is the way powerful nations have always behaved, and it is hard to see why the CIA has so often been blamed more than parallel agencies from other nations, such as Russia's KGB and France's DST.

Granted, politically aware people have always had good reason to question America's role as world policeman. Its intervention in Latin America last century led to the much satirized catchphrase "Yanqui go home!" The people in Latin America are almost all Catholic. Yet the citizens of Chile or Cuba or Bolivia who bitterly attacked US foreign policy did not consider that policy anti-Catholic. Some aspects of their anti-US narrative may have overlapped with the Muslim narrative now—notably what they saw as US greed and expansionism—but the fact that those who suffered from US interference happened to be Catholic had nothing to do with shaping the policy. Many of the places in the world where shots regrettably need to be fired in the twenty-first century happen to be Muslim. If an American administration decides that Marines have to be sent there, or CIA agents planted, that is no evidence of any anti-Muslim conspiracy.

The US has intervened many times in places with no oil and no strategic importance to speak of, such as Haiti, Somalia and Bosnia (the latter two in support of Muslims). In 2011 the US supported the side of Alassane Ouattara, from the Muslim north of the country, in the civil war in Ivory Coast. Muslims who follow the standard anti-US narrative naturally have little interest in Ivorian politics. However, if the US had happened to side with Ouattara's non-Muslim opponent Laurent Gbagbo, they would all have become experts. This is how the narrative works.

Unlike Europe, the US does not rely very heavily on Gulf oil. It now imports twice the amount of crude from Canada as from Saudi Arabia, which has recently fallen to third place behind Mexico. Muslims also should wonder why, if the US has stolen resources from Muslims, the Muslim Gulf oil states have become so wealthy. Clearly, they long ago shook off any US domination of their oil industries and have become richer per head than the US itself is. The Economist magazine estimated that Saudi investors alone lost around a trillion dollars when some of their investments in the USA collapsed during the recent recession. This was of course bad news for those investors, but it does show that Muslim oil-producing nations are hardly victims of US greed.

Wars cost the US money and blood. President Obama recently estimated the cost of the Iraq and A fghanistan wars at around 1.3 trillion dollars, and suggested that they have been the main reason for the economic recession. The notion that the US gains financially from war has little basis in fact. Naturally, some companies benefit from war, and much has been made of the cynical role Halliburton and its then subsidiary KBR played in the war in Iraq. However, the credit earned by such individual companies, massive though it may seem, is dwarfed by the debit which these wars have caused to the US economy as a whole. This effect is so pervasive that war can never be sensibly pursued as a matter of economic policy–a charge that many Muslims make against the US. The US no doubt looks after its own interests, in economic as in other matters. This is true in the sense that, like any other country in history, it would be foolish to act against its own interests. But there is nothing necessarily imperialistic about that, especially when what the US economy needs is peace.

A central part of the Muslim narrative against the US is that it somehow gains from keeping citizens of other nations–especially Muslim nations–poor and downtrodden. It is hard to see how that can be the case. As mentioned above, recent wars have cost the US vast amounts of money. How much better it would be for the US economy if the downtrodden in these countries were affluent enough to buy coveted American products: the Nikes, the Dells, the Chicken McNuggets. Those who buy into the standard narrative reply that the US has a war economy which thrives on weapons sales. Yet this is an odd claim: however vast its military machine, its non-military machine, which thrives on peace, dwarfs it.

International politics and economics are fantastically complex, and anyone who claims to have picked a philosophical path through it all must, if she is honest, add a rider that says "or maybe the opposite." The ideas I have expressed here on world affairs are based on reading the facts as I understand them. An expert in subtleties of espionage or the international arms trade may have convincing evidence that knocks all the claims of this chapter into a cocked hat. Yet the fact that these opinions may be wrong is not the point. Almost all those Muslims who unquestioningly follow the standard anti-Western narrative know less than I do about what is happening across the world, and many would hardly know a Kurd from a Kuwaiti. They therefore have even less reason for certainty than I have, and they cling to the "Muslims as victims" line for reasons that appear more psychological than logical.

An Association of Jews and Muslims

Soon after I became president of Muslims Against Terrorism (MAT) in 2002, I started attending various interfaith gatherings and meetings in Canada and the United States. It was at the Islamic Society of North America (ISNA) mosque where I first met Barbara Heller, a Jewish attendee of that interfaith event. She informed me about a vibrant Jewish-Muslim group in Toronto and invited me to attend the monthly meetings of this important association of Jews and Muslims.

The Canadian Association of Jews and Muslims met at the Toronto synagogue called Temple Emanuel. Rabbi Debra Landsberg was its official rabbi. The association had a Jewish head, Dr. Barbara Landau, and a Muslim head, Mr Shahid Akhtar. There were other people I had already come to know through my activism who were members of this group, including Tarek Fatah, Mark Persaud and Jeff Brown of the Unitarian Congregation in Mississauga, of which I was briefly director of religious education.

Although the Association was primarily a forum for members of the Muslim and Jewish community to discuss ideas and exchange cultural activities, there were also a few charitable causes the Association undertook. Products made by Palestinian farmers were sometimes displayed at the meetings. Additionally, fundraisers were at times organized to finance public events such as the Tikkum conference. Often some of us members were asked to speak on various topics the two co-chairs would choose, with the help of the members.

I was to conduct a three-day workshop along with Rabbi Debra Landsberg to discuss the role of both Muslim and Jewish women, the common challenges they faced as female members of orthodox faith communities, and how they had overcome some of these challenges. The three-day workshop was well attended and clarified many issues for both communities. Well-known attendees of the workshop included Dr. Karen Mock and Dr. Hussain Khilji. This was above all a learning opportunity for Jews and Muslims alike. How do Jewish women attain a measure of equality, at least within the Reform branch of Judaism? How can Muslim women overcome some of the theological challenges toward attaining gender equality within Islam? How do Jewish women interpret religious texts to their advantage and how can Muslim women learn from such approaches?

Both Rabbi Landsberg and I were convinced there was a move within religious communities toward fundamentalist readings of scripture. In this context the issue of veiling and segregation came up frequently. The issue of divorce among Muslim and Jewish women was another troubling issue that we both attempted to address. Rabbi Landsberg and I also discussed women in scripture and how some of the positive depictions of female religious figures could be used to the benefit of contemporary Muslim and Jewish women. I spoke about Khadijah, the prophet's first wife, who was also his employer.

Many other issues were also frequently discussed during the association's meetings. The relationship of Jews and Muslims as diaspora communities, and how they could come to each other's help in times of crisis, seemed to be a favourite with the members. What are some of the cultural initiatives that could be taken to bring the two communities together? It was decided that interesting Muslim and Jewish speakers of goodwill would be invited to speak at the meetings from time to time.

I remember that on one occasion I took my mother to the meetings to speak about her visit to Israel. My mother had visited Israel with my younger brother in the early nineties. She had always wanted to visit the Muslim sites, especially the al Aqsa mosque, or the dome of the rock, from where the prophet Mohammad is supposed to have ascended to the heavens in his famous night journey.

She told members of the congregation that she had enjoyed every moment of that visit, that she had felt welcomed there by the local Israeli population. She visited the church of the Holy Sepulchre in Bethlehem, she visited Hebron, or "al Khalil", as the Arab population called the town. She recalled how she was well-treated by local Israelis. She also said that she enjoyed the local cuisine. My mother was a big hit at the Association meeting. Later on, Barbara Landau came and told me that my mother was a *mensch*.

On another occasion, the co-chairs of the group organized a "Samoan circle". That was arranged in order for people to go around a circle and vent their true feelings without opposition. This was a way of dealing with pent-up emotions. The co-chairs informed us that this was also a method of compassionate listening, to develop empathy for the viewpoint of the opponent. Needless to say, some of the Palestinian and Muslim participants of the Samoan circle expressed their anger over the Israel-Arab conflict. Members of the Association had often noted that tensions between members of the two religious communities simmered over many issues. A conference would be organized to address these very sensitive matters using lectures and joint initiatives. That conference never materialized.

Even during the regular monthly meetings at the Temple Emanuel, Palestinians were invited to express their particular political objectives. Many of them offered the idea of a secular one-state solution. It was certainly a popular idea with some Palestinians, as eventually the demographics would turn in their favour. At that point I was in favour of a two-state solution. I upheld this view until later, when I became a member of the Muslim Canadian Congress, as the Congress endorses that solution. My opinion changed somewhat from that position after examining some historical accounts and opinions on this issue.

There are twenty-two Arab states, with tiny Israel in their midst. What is the problem? I have known Arabs to be very warm and hospitable people, but when it comes to acknowledging Jews as their neighbours, their blood begins to boil. Is this because Islamic hadith literature is replete with condemnation of the Jews? Why the inveterate hatred? Why can't Israel exist alongside Arab states? This does not mean I do not empathize with the disenfranchised Palestinian people. I certainly do, but I also feel that they are themselves partly responsible for their plight. They even rejected Ehud Barak's offer to establish a state in the West Bank and Gaza, which met a substantial portion of their demands.

I also firmly believe that the Palestinians will have to renounce terror to achieve their goal of establishing a state. Israel has an obligation to defend its innocent citizens from suicide bombers. Israelis face a continual threat of annihilation from the radical elements in certain segments of Palestinian society. Radical Muslims are driven by an apocalyptic zeal that sees as its end results the destruction of Israel and the demise of all other competing worldviews, including Western ideologies.

The Jewish people have undeniable historical links to the land called Palestine, as do the Arabs from the seventh century. Co-existence should be possible; the Arabs could recognize Israel and start an era of peaceful co-existence and mutual benefit. Some members of the Association suggested that this was a political and territorial war, not a religious one. But the warring parties saw themselves as distinct religious communities, and this was surely the basis of the dispute.

I visited Barbara Landau on one occasion and told her that the Jewish people had every right to establish their own homeland, as that is the only place that would guarantee them security as a very tiny religious community on the world scale. She said I was one of the few Muslims she had met who were "pro-Israel". I told her that I was also pro-Palestinian and wished the Palestinian people to have the same security and dignity as the Israelis.

Another cultural event organized by the Association was the annual multi-faith sedar. We all brought our stories of personal struggles and liberation from these struggles to the table as we broke unleavened bread together. The multi-faith sedars were social events we all looked forward to during the year. As a reciprocal gesture, some Muslim members hosted Eid and Ramadan dinners for Jewish friends.

On one occasion our Jewish friends requested a visit to a mosque. The Muslim members of this association were hosted monthly in a synagogue, so it was natural for the Jewish members to want to visit a mosque at least once. Since my husband is a long-time supporter of the ISNA Canada mosque, he volunteered to arrange this visit for our Jewish friends. Barbara Landau, Sy Landau, Barbara Heller, and other Jewish friends were all very excited.

We advised them about the dress code and other mosque protocols. No shoes in the prayer area, no speaking during prayer, no touching the Quran except when clean. Our Jewish friends readily understood all this, as they show similar reverence to the Torah. Mr Khalid was arranged to be our host for the day. We all arrived at the ISNA mosque together–both the Jewish and Muslim members of this excited group.

Mr Khalid welcomed the group warmly. He gave the group a synopsis of Islamic beliefs and practices. Our Jewish friends were encouraged to ask any questions. We were then offered some refreshments and were called into the prayer area to observe the method of congregational prayer. There is an imam who leads the prayer. The congregation bows when he bows; they kneel when he kneels. The men all stand in the front rows and there is a partition between the men's and the women's rows.

I saw Barbara Landau attempting to perform the prayer. Her hair was covered and she appeared worshipful. Some of the Muslim attendees chose to remain outside the prayer hall. They had chosen not to pray. An hour's discussion on Jewish/Muslim issues followed the prayer. Various possible initiatives were discussed, including a Tikkun conference led by Rabbi Michael Lerner. The feasibility of "twinning" mosques and synagogues was considered. In this, the Noor Cultural Centre of Toronto, a progressive Muslim group, would team up with the local synagogues.

Some Muslims at the mosque commented on how Meir Kahane, the ultra-nationalist Israeli rabbi, had allegedly ordered the killings of all Palestinians. The issue of the Protocol of the Learned Elders of Zion was also mentioned. While some of the Muslim members of the mosque tried to tell these misinformed Muslims that the Protocol was forged, many refused to believe this. The issue of disproportionate killings of Palestinians came up. The occupation, the refugees, the lack of Israeli acknowledgement of the Palestinian right of return were all thorny issues that could not have been avoided. In the end, some of our Jewish friends left with the feeling that perhaps they should never have come to the mosque. They felt that the accepted narrative there was one-sided and that all Jews were being judged according to Meir Kahane's standards.

The group did not achieve much that night. The idea was to build bridges. Instead we returned with the feeling that the problems facing the two religious communities were too profound to be addressed in forums such as the one offered by the Canadian Association of Jews and Muslims.

Many began to wonder if interfaith groups like these served any purpose at all, but I disagreed. Without such dialogue, Muslim and Jew would never look each other in the eye as equals. These groups at least served the purpose of keeping people of goodwill together in endorsing a principled stand and in disseminating more tolerant views in their respective faith communities. I joined similar groups and joint initiatives in Mississauga. The Credit Valley Interfaith group and the 905 faith leaders' meetings were important in uniting members of faith communities.

Then came the fighting between Israel and Lebanon in 2006. Both the Muslim Canadian Congress and the Canadian Association of Jews and Muslims issued statements urging restraint on both sides. Hezbollah soon began to take charge of the war and were firing Katushya rockets into Israel. One morning we heard of the civilian deaths in Qana and we were all saddened by the loss of innocent lives there. The MCC was swift in issuing a statement on the Qana tragedy. But the Muslim Canadian Congress faced a challenge of its own at that time. Some members left the MCC, thinking our stand on the Israel/Hezbollah war was not a principled one, as these members firmly held the Israelis to be the aggressors. On that and other issues, the MCC split into two organizations, the Muslim Canadian Congress and the Canadian Muslim Union. I became chair of the Muslim Canadian Congress at that time.

It was also around that time that the Canadian Association of Jews and Muslims began to lose members. The issues were too deep-rooted to be resolved by a small interfaith alliance. Members held no illusions of being able to solve international problems, but had rather brought with them old grievances that would fester for a while. In time the Muslim members went their way and the Jewish members theirs. Meetings became infrequent. While the Canadian Association of Jews and Muslims still exists, its activities are now mostly confined to issuing press releases. The organization also continues to offer good wishes on Eid, Ramadan and Jewish festivals, but other than arranging some mosque and synagogue "twinnings" there remains little activism in the Association.

I forged independent friendship with some of my Jewish colleagues around that time. Rabbi Larry Englander, who has served the Solel Congregation in Mississauga for a long time, was also originally a member of the Jewish Muslim group. He became a good friend. I have given talks at the Solel congregation many times, handling some of the issues that affect both religious communities. Once I ran into some difficulty explaining certain Quranic texts to the Jewish audience.

The most contentious of these was the one that mentioned God having punished the Jews (by turning them into apes) for breaking the Sabbath. I attempted to suggest that the Quran merely spoke of the Jews of the time, and only one particular group of them who had broken the Sabbath. I pointed out other verses that spoke of Jews as the people of the book, who were of a kindred religious community. A member of the audience replied that if that was the best Islam's holy book could say about the Jews, it was not enough! Others also asked awkward and searching questions about Islam, such as why Muslims appeared so easily corrupted. At that time, the only answer that came to me was that Muslims were caught in the midst of many political conflicts and were simply angry. I realize the inadequacy of that answer now. I now believe that the problem lies within Islamic historical texts and hadith literature. No doubt contemporary conflicts have exacerbated the problem, but the problem lies squarely in the ideology of Islamism.

Arliene Botnick, the educator at the Solel congregation, had also invited me to speak at the luncheon events of the synagogue. I took the opportunity to condemn all the violence against diaspora Jews and innocent Israeli citizens as well as other terrorism across the world. I felt that Muslims had not done enough to condemn extremism. The throngs that we needed to see on the streets condemning violence in the name of Islam were absent.

I felt very welcomed during my visits to the Solel congregation. I even brought my family members to visit the congregation, to look at the Torah, to participate in many of the Sabbath services. Open dialogue was always encouraged, even on the most contentious issues.

Through Larry Englander I also joined other interfaith alliances that were doing community work, relieving poverty, engaging in charity initiatives and promoting a narrative that would build bridges between communities living in Canada. Through Arliene Botnick, I also met Judy Csillag, prominent journalist Ron Csillag's older sister. Along with a Christian delegate, we were soon to leave for Syria to conduct citizen diplomacy among Jewish, Christian and Muslim populations in that now war-ravaged country.

Syria was calm and peaceful at that time. Everyone seemed to get along. At that point it was hard to sense any underlying resentment toward the Assad regime. We arrived in Damascus in January 2009. I was a guest of Pegatha Taylor, then diplomatic envoy to Syria from Canada. Judy and Kathy were guests of our friend Hind Kabawat, the organizer of the conference, in which "citizen diplomacy" would be conducted. The conference was largely attended by Syrian women lawyers, journalists, academics and activists. There was a general sense of wanting to accomplish something good for the three communities, and women were to be trained as leaders toward this end. Many workshops were conducted during those meetings. Stories were exchanged and grievances heard.

In the evenings, Judy, Kathy, Hind and I would roam the market or *sooq*. But anti-Israel sentiment was quite palpable on the streets. The war between Gaza and Israel was raging at that time. The figures on the screen showed Israel's military might as a kind of grisly scoreboard: 13 Israeli dead against 313 Palestinians. During our visit, Judy and I also stumbled upon people trampling on a drawing of the Israeli flag on the street. Naturally Judy, being Jewish, felt very uncomfortable. On another occasion, we came upon a Syrian shopkeeper who was cursing the Israeli army. At the conference, some women declared "We don't hate Jews. We just hate the Zionists." All over the streets of Damascus was the catchphrase "Gaza bleeds".

The conference itself was a success, but once again we left with the sense that the issues were far too complex for any lasting goodwill to be engendered among the groups. I was an active member of these groups until fall of 2009, when I fell seriously ill and had to undergo emergency surgery. In time these groups disintegrated.

Why are Muslims Intolerant?

Many movies, cartoons and writings that emerge in the Western world certainly offend Muslims. Much of what is written against Christianity also offends some pious Christians. However, people who cause such offence should not pay with their lives, and it is questionable whether they should even be prevented from speaking their minds.

Ever since 9/11, there have been several protests in the Islamic world over the actions of individual Westerners who simply exercised their right to free speech. They make movies of the prophet Mohammad as they make movies of Christ, Noah and Moses. If *The Ten Commandments* depicts Moses as a killer, should Jews then take up arms against Hollywood? For more than a hundred years, there has been objective nonreligious analysis of the historical facts of the Bible. Even the most devout Christian living in the West would not question a person's right to subject the Bible to such scrutiny. No such "higher criticism" of the Quran on the other hand has ever been proliferated, for fear of Muslim anger. If Muslims can scrutinize the Bible, Christians should be able to question the historical truth of the Quran.

Mere rumours of Quran burnings or insults to the prophet ignite the Muslim world into a frenzy of violence and hysteria. Gillian Gibbons, a 54-year-old British schoolteacher, was suddenly arrested in Sudan in November, 2007. Her "crime" was to allow her class of nine-year-olds to name their class toy, a cute and cuddly stuffed brown teddy bear, "Mohammed ". This must be a Western conspiracy, concluded the mobs who gathered to demand Gibbon's head for committing the ultimate blasphemy. While Gibbons escaped the threats, poor decapitated Theo van Gogh's body had already been buried for releasing *Submission*, a film deemed "anti-Islam". And of course, the manufactured rage against urbane and peaceful Denmark over the Jyllands-Posten cartoons of Mohammed will never be forgotten.

Iftekhar Hai, the moderate Muslim I consulted about Feisal Shahzad, the New York car bomber, believes Islam encourages respect for diversity and he often quotes verses of the Quran to support his claim. He often refers to the verse from Chapter 49: Verse 13, which states that God did not create diversity among nations so people would despise each other but that "they may know each other".

And yet one finds the following Quranic verse as well: "Allah hath purchased of the believers their persons and their goods; for theirs (in return) is the garden (of Paradise): they fight in His cause, and slay and are slain: A promise binding on Him in truth, through the Law, the Gospel, and the Quran" (Quran 9:111)

Radical Muslims will say that the cause for which Muslims must fight includes protection of dogma, as God's final message to humankind must be defended and preserved at all costs. This is the ultimate good that any human being or any Muslim can strive for. To die in the cause of Allah is in fact the ultimate moral act from an ultraconservative Islamic standpoint. From this mindset, any assaults on the purity of the faith must be protested.

Recently there was also uproar about an innocuous and amateurish movie allegedly made by an Israeli Jew (but actually a Coptic Christian). This movie, *The Innocence of Muslims*, depicts the prophet of Islam as a lascivious man given to buffoonery. It also portrays him as a homosexual. I know that many Muslims in the GTA were upset and offended. I too was offended. But so what? Non-Muslims have the right to assert their non-belief as vehemently as they desire. I was asked to comment on this on CTV in Toronto. I said that the protesting radicals need to understand that non-believers have no reason to respect Muslim beliefs or to apologize for their own unbelief. Why was the Coptic movie maker under any obligation to show reverence to the prophet of Islam? This was his opinion and he had the right to express it, even if his movie was inaccurate and inept.

Historical accounts confirm that the prophet did indeed have multiple wives, which makes it all the less likely that he was a homosexual. But no matter what the content of the movie, and whether it was made by an Israeli or a Coptic Christian, it was a mistake to give it any attention. It would have been long forgotten if it had simply been ignored. But Muslims across the world began to burn tires, smash windows and bay for infidel blood.

Even in North America some organizations called for peaceful protests against the movie. They fail to understand that although people live their religion through life and ritual, religions are also belief systems, which people must be free to accept or reject. It is perfectly acceptable for people who do not subscribe to such ideas to challenge them as vehemently as they like. If the faithful are sincere and resolute in their own belief, there is no reason why the unbelief of others should upset them.

A typical Muslim response to the notion of freedom of conscience is that religions should be spared denigration. Yet any religious beliefs should be open to scrutiny, criticism and even abuse—and especially those that are obviously oppressive. Some specific religious practices certainly need to attract criticism, such as the belief that women ought to be circumcised. Girls as young as five and six have suffered serious health hazards because of this practice. Polygamy greatly disadvantages women, so why must it not be subjected to intense scrutiny and criticism? Even if Muslims believe in it, non-Muslims have no reason to stifle their opposition.

Theo Van Gogh, Punjab governor Salman Taseer and countless unnamed others are now all dead at the hands of others who were defending dogma. The belief that freedom of speech must stop at religion is fairly widespread in the Islamic world. It flourishes even among the educated upper class in many countries, including Pakistan. Yet the victims are not only those Westerners who are threatened; such a reaction also turns Muslims themselves into victims, because such a "wag the dog" reaction distracts them from what really needs to change in their world. Why do Muslims have to be so thin-skinned as to fall for this every time? Many Muslims see such attacks on Islam as part of a coordinated Western conspiracy against Islam, yet Western cultural and religious icons get the same treatment. Films such as *The Last Temptation of Christ, Religulous* and *Dogma* have challenged core Christian beliefs.

Muslims, too, often denigrate other belief systems, and do not refrain from mocking and disparaging members of other faith communities. Cartoons of Jews and Christians abound in the Islamic world. They often claim that they never attack the beliefs of others or denigrate the prophets of others. This claim needs to be addressed. Muslims ostensibly consider all previous prophets to have been inspired by God. Moses, Jesus, David, Abraham and Noah are all revered prophets in Islam.

They regard all the Biblical prophets as being sent by the one true God. According to this view, all prophets basically brought the same message to mankind; there is only one God and true religion requires submission to that God. This in essence is the meaning of Islam. Hence, according to mainstream Islam, all religions in their true form resemble Islam and were distorted over the centuries. It is therefore incumbent on Muslims to respect and revere all the Biblical prophets. Some also hold that non-Biblical prophets like Krishna and Zoroaster may have also received the same divine message. Therefore Muslims should not make pictures of other prophets, ridicule them or challenge their legitimacy.

Muslims therefore feel greatly insulted when non-Muslims criticize the prophet Mohammad. They are particularly anguished when they see "the people of the book" i.e. Jews and Christians, making fun of Mohammad because they expect total reciprocity from their cousins in belief. They feel betrayed when they themselves do not criticize Noah or Moses but Mohammad becomes the subject of ridicule.

The problem also lies in the difference in understanding of the term "prophet". Within Islam, the prophet is the most revered figure–one that receives inspiration from God directly. This has to be a very special person. To challenge such a person is like committing a great heresy. Muslims therefore do not understand that in the Western world, prophets are first of all thought of as ordinary human beings who may be men of God, but are also capable of all the human follies. To challenge aspects of their character, to disparage some of their pronouncements or even to challenge their beliefs is never an issue.

But despite the nominal proscription on belittling other beliefs, Muslims show no restraint in criticizing or mocking the beliefs of non-Muslims. The Christian trinity is attacked, Hindu polytheism is denigrated, Sikhism is ridiculed. While it is true that Biblical personalities are never criticized, the Bible itself is dismissed as having been corrupted, and the Hindu Vedas are labelled mythology pure and simple. It is therefore disingenuous for Muslims to assert that they brook no mockery of other world faiths.

In the West, people believe in this openness because mankind has ultimately benefited from it. Certain religious practices like polygamy that oppress women are hence illegal in the West, whereas in Islamic countries, no one would dare challenge such a practice, as it would be seen as sanctioned by the Quran. There is therefore an enormous difference in mindset between Westerners and Muslims. In order to dispel the resentment this argument generates, one would have to urge Muslims to understand that there is no Western conspiracy against Islam; the way freedom of expression is understood in the West allows all beliefs to be questioned, and Westerners openly challenge and even ridicule beliefs they traditionally cherished.

It is not just for Westerners that fundamentalist Muslims demonstrate intolerance. Even divergent ideas and notions from within the faith are shunned.

Muslims like me, who advocate a more liberal strain, are often deemed non-Muslim or even traitors. Fatwas of apostasy are often hurled at such Muslims. Minority sects are hated by the majority. Muslims from the Ahmedia sect of Islam, for example, have been castigated as outsiders. They have been declared a non-Muslim minority in Pakistan and they are often hunted and attacked in countries like Bangladesh.

This issue is, as so many are, a highly sensitive one. Mainstream Islam believes that Mohammad was the last of all messengers of God in a long line of prophets, some of whom are recognized by Judaism and Christianity. The founder of the Ahmedia sect, Mirza Ghulam Ahmed, claimed that he too was a latter-day prophet and had come to revive the true sharia of Mohammad. According to mainstream Islam, such a claim violates Islam's core belief.

However, I have often argued that the Ahmedia believe in Islam's central doctrine: monotheism. They disagree only on an issue that has not been expounded in the Quran and does not even constitute one of the so-called five pillars of Islam. Muslims should therefore not repudiate a minority sect which agrees with them on a central issue.

Divergence of opinion even within a religion must be cherished rather than shunned. Such divergence is how oppressive practices, misogynistic interpretations and unjust laws will eventually be discarded. That is how one can hope for some positive change in Muslim societies. The same is true of accommodating the beliefs of other minority sects within Islam, such as the various branches of Shia. Furthermore, the calls of modernist and reformist Muslims from any sect of Islam must be heeded and embraced. Modernist Muslims wish to see Muslim societies progress and prosper. They must not be viewed with suspicion. Intolerance is counter-productive. It thwarts progress by stifling thought, research and inquiry. The result is the kind of stagnation that one so often sees in contemporary Muslim societies.

I completed my doctorate in education in 2010 and wrote a dissertation on incorporating inclusive and liberal ideas within a religious curriculum that both secular schools (where religious education is mandatory in Islamic countries) as well as the madrassahs or religious seminaries could adopt. I interviewed twenty participants for this study. These were academics, activists, scholars and lay people interested in the education system of Pakistan, where the recent trend has been to send children to religious schools because of the free room and board they offer.

The people I interviewed for my study were Muslims and ex Muslims. Some of them believed that tolerance was an integral part of Islamic teaching and a cherished Islamic value. They expressed hope that Islam's own tradition of tolerance would solve its problems. They believed Islam had been hijacked by the fundamentalists and to some extent the orthodoxy–an opinion they shared with most moderate Muslims. They believed that man-made sharia law and political Islam were actually a bastardized version of Islam and did it more disservice than benefit.

Some of the more liberal and agnostic interviewees believed that much needed to be expunged from Islamic belief. They would have excised all the verses on jihad, warfare, *dhimmi* tax, the treatment of women and minorities and the treatment of slaves. One interviewee said that religion should be taught to children by parents and caregivers and has no place in schools. Religious and spiritual education, if it should be mandatory in schools at all, should entail taking the best elements of Islam and incorporating them in an ethical and civic curriculum that will foster tolerance, harmony and peaceful attitudes among Muslims.

Unless education authorities end the exclusionary and elitist attitude that is now part of the curriculum in Islamic schools, the indoctrination of Muslims will continue, and Muslims will not stop viewing the world arrogantly and parochially. They will continue to despise the Jews and Hindus, they will continue to be suspicious of Christians, even while trying to migrate to nominally Christian lands to avail themselves of the economic opportunities. They will continue to stifle dissenting Muslim voices.

Civic education advocating values of tolerance and harmony is therefore the answer to the Muslim world's intolerance. But this will not be accomplished overnight. Civil groups certainly work hard to advance a more modern narrative among the masses, but the obscurantist clerics are ever-present to thwart their efforts. Little wonder that the blasphemy laws in Pakistan have not been repealed and have no chance even of being amended. Sherry Rahman, current Pakistani ambassador to the US, had attempted to introduce amendments to the law, at the very least to require an intent to commit a crime of blasphemy. Even that was shouted down.

The current climate of most Muslim countries, including Pakistan, Bangladesh, Iran and Afghanistan, does not tolerate any divergence from the ultraconservative religious view. The Ahmedis, the Shia and non-Muslim communities continue to suffer as a result. I have often written in support of these minority groups and have consequently also suffered rebuke from both family and friends.

Islam and Music: a Conflict Within

At times I have felt that my religion and the greatest passion of my life, music, were at complete odds.

Islamic literature is contradictory about whether it tolerates music. I could never tell if music was truly *haram*, as the fundamentalists asserted. As a child, I began a formal study of music with my teacher, Mrs Mary Elizabeth Henderson. It was her commitment to teaching, as well as her passionate interest in me as a student, that inculcated in me a deep love of Western classical music. I had also grown up listening to this genre of music from my English grandmother. My two paternal aunts and father were also accomplished pianists. Now was my chance to learn the same type of music and I immersed myself in a study of piano technique and music theory with great alacrity.

Betty Henderson was herself a very talented pianist. She had at one time been the student of concert pianist Lilly Dumont, who was best known for her renditions of Mozart. Lilly Dumont's interpretations would be imparted to me through one of her most able students–my teacher Betty.

Betty introduced me to the best piano repertoire: exquisite Beethoven sonatas, cheerful Mozart minuets, Scarlatti's delightful single movement sonatas, Haydn's playful tunes and Bach's preludes, fugues, sinfonias and inventions. I wanted to play them all. I was quite voracious at learning new pieces every time I went for my weekly piano lessons.

All this was wonderfully exciting for me.

But anxiety about whether I should pursue my passion often lurked at the back of my mind. Soon after performing the Hajj in 2002, I experienced a phase of fervid religiosity that intensified the conflict within me. At that point I even thought of giving up music. There was considerable suspicion of music among committed Muslims around me. I had heard many negative comments about the "immorality" of music from clerics as well as family and friends. This gave rise to the conflict in my mind about whether or not I should pursue music even as a hobby. Was I sinning against Islam? I had heard all sorts of hadith about music being the source of all that was lustful and immoral. On one occasion, a local cleric narrated a hadith stating that the prophet Mohammad had been sent into this world for no other reason than to destroy musical instruments. Really? Not to preach a particular brand of monotheism or to expound or to create a just society?

Music had always been a source of comfort for me. I seriously questioned the validity of these hadith. It would eventually lead me to discard most hadith literature as spurious. It would also force me to investigate the authenticity of Islam's accepted historical narratives. Whatever my inner conflict, it did not deter me from continuing to develop musically. When I started university, I also registered in college level music courses on theory, harmony and counterpoint. I came to Canada in 1984 and continued my musical studies here. I registered with the Mississauga School of Music and was once again very lucky to have a talented teacher, a Pole by the name of Garagina. Soon I was ready to take the Royal Conservatory of Music's examinations for piano and theory.

I continued practicing Islam as best as I could and also continued with my study of music. This was also the time that my two sons were attending the Islamic school. What was absent from the school curriculum was music as a subject. Instead children were learning *tajweed*, a special rhythmic way of reciting the Quran.

The school once put up an event that was to depict Islamic stories from the past through drama. Again there was some singing, but it all had to take place without music or instrumental accompaniment. I once again questioned the absence of musical instruments. When my older son was in grade five and my younger son in grade three, they had been transferred to the neighbourhood public school. I started instructing my two boys in piano technique. At three, my daughter was still too young to begin musical study.

I also began to volunteer at the public school my sons attended. There I met a young Muslim boy, who said his family did not allow him to attend music class. He was convinced music was *haram* or prohibited. That was an extreme view but I had heard it expressed by other members of the community, including close friends and family.

Indeed in Islam, all sorts of taboos exist against music. One of my relative's is a *tablighi* or Muslim evangelical. What he once remarked to me was shocking. He told me I should quit playing Haydn, Mozart and Beethoven. They were all *kafirs,* or people who rejected the oneness of God or the prophethood of Mohammad. Puzzled, I asked him how he came to that conclusion. He said it was simply that they were not Muslims and music is a *gunah kabira,* or a very grave sin. Something so intellectually stimulating and good for the human soul was a *gunah kabira*?

That opinion would be confirmed by a long-time friend who had turned into a religious fundamentalist. She had at one time also started wearing the niqab but had recently given it up as she was now "past the child-bearing age" and the prescription on how she was supposed to dress had been relaxed. Just like my *tablighi* relative, she thought that music was indeed the voice of Satan. This was how Satan would beguile Muslims and lure them away from the worship of Allah.

Then recently we heard of twelve Muslim families who sought exemption for their children from compulsory music and physical education classes in Manitoba schools. These families obviously practise an ultraconservative brand of Islam; they wish to indoctrinate the next generation of Muslims into rejecting music and therefore a major part of what is vibrant and ennobling about Canadian public school education. As a Muslim who has taught music to Canadian children, I was naturally curious to examine the accuracy of these ultra-conservative opinions on music from a strictly Islamic perspective. What exactly do the Quran and hadith say about music? What are some of the opinions of Islamic scholars on the issue?

I had initially embarked on a study of Islamic texts to seek some answers primarily to resolve the conflict about the suitability of music, a conflict that often tore me apart. I have now made peace within my conscience, as I no longer feel bound by contradictory religious texts. Should Muslims rely on literature that is replete with inconsistencies, contradictions and ambiguities? However, prior to this realization, I had sent for the well-known book entitled *The Lawful and the Prohibited in Islam* by the Islamist cleric Sheikh Mohammad al Qaradawi.

Not surprisingly, the Quran is silent on the issue. Therefore, individuals prohibiting music rely mostly on hadith, a body of literature that suffers from countless contradictions. Some hadith appear to proscribe music, while others clearly allow its use. Sheikh Qaradawi considers music permissible if it agrees with Islamic morals. He believes it is acceptable if it is not exciting.

Unveiled:

I did not understand what he meant by music not being exciting. Was he talking about music having sexual content? Perhaps. But music that is not in some sense exciting is not really music. Were Muslims to listen only to music which had been drained of its very essence?

Qaradawi had gone a step further and cited many hadith from Bukhari, the compendium of hadith that is regarded as the most authentic. He quoted the hadith where the prophet Mohammad had permitted music and singing at a wedding. Typical of hadith literature, other hadith conflicted with this one. One stated the following:

"There will be a people from my ummah (nation) who will seek to make lawful fornication, the wearing of silk, wine drinking and the use of music instruments."[1].

A scholar named al Kanadi had given a detailed explanation of this hadith. He said that according to this hadith even singing *a cappella* was not permitted. This was like taking my life's breath away. I had always enjoyed singing, even as a child. That was how my mother had discovered my musical talent. Was I to sing only hymns of praise and the *nasheed* that most Muslims believed was permitted? *Nasheed* were simply songs in praise of the prophet Mohammad to be sung *a cappella*.

Those who wish to establish a general prohibition against music consider Qaradawi's opinions to be based on dubious research. The consensus among moderate Muslims, however, is that Islam prohibits music only in instances where there is a chance of exploitation. This explains why the prophet of Islam cautioned against the misuse of music, if he did at all. Women and young girls in the Arabia of his time were often sold into prostitution and then made to sing and dance provocatively in public. But that can hardly be a fear in Canada's elementary schools, whether or not Muslim families prevent their children from attending music class. Other hadith on the restricted permissibility of music include the prophet's youngest wife Ayesha's statement that he allowed singing and playing the drum on Eid.

Orthodoxy has interpreted this hadith to mean that music is permitted in a limited sort of way and on special occasions. But this begs the question as to why the prophet would allow something that is contradictory to Islamic values even as an exception. Such logic suggests that even adultery may be allowed on special occasions. We know that is certainly not the case. Some more liberal Muslim scholars suggest that only music leading to other vices, such as prostitution, is prohibited. They say that it all depends on the intent, and any activity can be abused in this manner. They are surely right: even the most benign of activities can be turned into an exploitative practice.

Another hadith also alluded to the notion that deeds would be judged according to intentions. Certainly, if music were to result in the exploitation of women, children or other marginalized groups, then its intention and impact would have to be questioned.

Music by and large is played for personal pleasure. In my years as a music teacher, I have taught children from all ethnic and religious backgrounds. I have also taught Muslim children–even hijabi ones! Surely they would have been shocked to learn that what they were doing offended the spirit of Islam.

There have been recent attempts to involve Muslims in music in a restricted way. The Muslim community of greater Toronto has for some years organized a Muslim cultural festival called Muslimfest. No women are allowed to sing or perform in it, and if men sing they must do so only *a cappella* or with a *daf* (drum) as accompaniment. I have seen flyers for these festivals many times. It often includes the caption "Performances will be strictly in line with sharia".

Restricting instruments to the *daf* makes no clear sense in the twenty-first century. This was most likely the only readily available musical instrument in the time of the prophet of Islam. If the violin or piano existed over a thousand years ago in Arabia and the singing were accompanied by these instruments at the time, it would presumably then be permissible to use these instruments for accompaniment in modern Ontario. Allowing only an older version of the drum is simply too literal to be adopted as a sensible interpretation of Islamic precept.

Yet the same literal approach is employed to discourage the visual arts. I have looked through the Quran to find an explicit prohibition against painting and drawing. I have found none. The hadith prohibit depicting the prophet Mohammad or making physical representation of God, for fear of enabling idolatry. Even the Ten Commandments prohibit graven images. While that may be valid from a religious standpoint, it cannot be applied literally to all art forms. If intent is to be counted as a valid principle on which to base religious precept, then the intent of almost all art is not idolatry but simply creative expression. A physical representation of God is forbidden within Islam. By extension, a physical representation of the prophet Mohammad and his close companions would also be prohibited, in the interests of discouraging idolatry. But a mere flight of an artist's fancy is hardly something to be forbidden.

Art and music uplift our souls; they enable us to transcend the mundane. Music is also linked to greater intellectual achievement. Some studies have shown that the learning of music enhances intellectual capabilities, and children who learn musical instruments show an increase in IQ. Fundamentalist Muslim families fear the influence of music on their elementary schoolchildren, and seem unaware of the benefits of teaching music to young children.

**Part Three
Reflections**

The Contemporary Muslim World

Because of the internet and other uncensored media, Muslims are currently exposed to a more enlightened view of the world. Some are beginning to understand the true meaning of pluralism, egalitarianism, liberal democracy, freedom of speech and freedom of conscience. Some Muslims have recently even started tentatively to examine the origins of Islam and the historicity of the Quran in the light of modern archaeological findings and critical research. Many have recently begun to question their religion, as it has come to be greatly scrutinized in the crucible of 9/11.

These crucial research developments have had certain implications for the Islamic world. It appears that some Muslims have secretly renounced Islam, and avoided confrontation with family and friends by simply maintaining cultural ties to the faith. They are Muslims in the sense that some nominal Western Christians are Christian. These cultural Muslims celebrate Eid and participate in cultural activities shaped by Islam, but do not necessarily subscribe to its core beliefs. They choose not to declare their non-belief for fear of ostracism or even reprisals. It is therefore impossible to put a number on such nominal Muslims. However, the websites of active groups such as Faith Freedom International and Society of ex-Muslims suggest that there seems to be a movement toward disbelief among at least some people from the Muslim fold.

This trend can be seen especially among the educated who are either living in the West or are exposed to critical research and inquiry back in their homelands. The Muslim masses, on the other hand, are cloistered, uneducated and indoctrinated to the point where they do not brook any criticism whatsoever of Islamic belief and practice. It is these masses who participate in demonstrations against any perceived insults to Islam.

Many Muslims who question Islam have often secretly repudiated it. The masses, on the other hand, do not question its tenets. They therefore oppose introducing changes to modernize it. People also convert to Islam across the world, but they convert to the more orthodox brand of Islam.

There is therefore movement toward Islam and movement away from Islam, but mainstream Islam has remained orthodox. Liberal Muslims have not yet been able to provide a viable alternative that is more in synch with modern values and sensibilities. That is also partially why some Westerners convert to orthodox Islam. Some Western women seem to be taking to Islam's value system as they feel "protected" by it. They relish the segregation, or the fact that husbands are supposed to fend for their families, or that all Muslim women are responsible for is the home, children and family.

Pakistan, my country of origin, has also witnessed a resurgence of religiosity in recent years. Even the upper classes have turned religious. They were previously seduced by Western freedoms, but now prefer to send their children to schools where a strictly orthodox Islamic education is being imparted to children.

Members of my husband's extended family choose to send their daughters to these schools. The girls wear the hijab and abaya to school. They are not allowed to communicate with boys, as the environment is one of strict segregation. The Rosen Academy is one such school. Located in a posh locality in my home city of Lahore, the school offers a strictly orthodox curriculum. My two nephews also attended another elitist Islamist school in one of the suburbs of Lahore. There too the environment was strictly segregated. Political or fundamentalist Islam has therefore found its way into the more affluent classes that were once anglicized, at least during my childhood. The problem of Islamic fundamentalism is therefore not confined to religious seminaries, and the answer must be sought through a revamping of the educational system across the board.

This fundamentalism also has tentacles abroad. Some Muslims see propagating Islam as the very purpose of their presence in the West. A relation of mine who turned religious thinks that Muslim presence in the West is justified only if Muslims preach Islam here. They cannot live in non-Muslim "kafir" lands unless they take the opportunity to "convey God's message to mankind." He believes that without this objective, it would be "haram" or prohibited for Muslims to live in a land where they cannot dispense sharia law or live according to Islam's commandments. Perhaps that is why many orthodox Muslims living in Western countries like Canada demand outrageous faith accommodations like prayer halls in the public school system.

There is now definitely an emphasis on religious conformity despite the fact that Muslims across the world are a motley crowd. They are black, white, Asian, African, Chinese, European, and every conceivable blend. They are religious, secular, liberal, conservative, militant, peaceful, reclusive, gregarious, committed, and sometimes even cavalier about their faith. But as diverse as Muslims are in their religious predilections, the orthodox community believes it is mandated by God to keep Muslims on track. They must not stray from Islam's core beliefs. They believe there is only one Islam, and it needs to be preserved at all costs.

Such Muslims in the aftermath of 9/11 have either become overly defensive about their faith or immensely belligerent about any criticism of their beliefs and practices. Unfortunately, the rioting that occurs over perceived insults to Islam tower over other more tolerant strains of pure religious devotion within Islamic communities. Also, regrettably, the loudest voices tend to be the ones that abhor the West, despise progress, and have a romanticized view of Islam's history of conquest and domination.

Doubtless, Islamic civilization was at one time the leading civilization of the world. The Islamic learning centres of Cordoba in Spain in fact inspired other Europeans to come out of their state of inertia to explore the new ideas in fields such as economics, science and medicine. Islamic polities fostered vibrant communities that instilled a love of learning in all disciplines. Ancient Greek works were translated into Arabic. Neither time nor money was spared to build libraries, universities and hospitals across the Islamic empire.

These pre-renaissance achievements were indeed laudable, but the tide began to turn against Muslims after the Christian West, inspired by empiricism and its own ethics of hard work and enterprise, began a quest for achievement and expansion throughout the world. Contemporary Muslims still experience nostalgia about their lost glory. Many across the world contend that it is their abandonment of Islamic precept and practice that has precipitated the decline of their civilization and society.

The simple truth is that too many Muslims today are illiterate, backward and, in many countries, quite beleaguered. Apart from the oil-rich desert kingdoms, they have little political clout internationally. Their educational systems are outdated, sometimes following medieval madrassah-type curricula that evoke an era that has no relevance for modern times. According to the 2001 UNDP reports, literacy in Islamic countries overall was still less than sixty percent.

Unveiled:

In Muslim societies today there is general apathy and lack of initiative. For example, there have been few scientific achievements by Muslims in the last century. The political institutions of these countries remain archaic, and democracy has not taken root even in countries that aspire to be democratic. Pakistan has experimented with democracy, both the presidential and the parliamentary form, but has been plagued throughout its history by military coups and dictators who obstruct democratic forces. There seems to have been, up until now, little initiative by the Muslim masses to overthrow dictatorial regimes. In general, Muslims appear satisfied with tradition and maintaining the status quo.

While Muslims across the world still suffer from rampant illiteracy and backwardness, civil society has miraculously still managed to emerge in Muslim communities. It exists in Pakistan, Bangladesh, the Middle East, North Africa and everywhere else where Islam is the majority religion of the population. It is civil society that forms organizations to combat the inequalities embedded in sharia law. Organizations such as the Women's Action Forum in Pakistan have for decades protested abuses against women under the law. However, the wall of orthodoxy is a too formidable barrier for the aspirations of ordinary citizens in Pakistan and similar Muslim countries, despite the assistance such groups may offer. For this reason many Muslims who have the means to do so have migrated to Canada and other Western countries.

Muslims in Canada

Muslims in Canada are as diverse as the populations they have left behind in Islamic countries. Many of the civil society adherents have also made their way into Canada. While a significant number of Canadian Muslims support sharia, perhaps a greater number simply wish to live their lives peacefully and amicably with other Canadians, treating their religion as a personal matter.

Muslims constitute about 2.7 % of the Canadian population. About 65 % identify themselves as Sunni Muslims while about 15 % call themselves Shia Muslims. The remainder are either from the Ahmedia sect or call themselves secular or non-practicing Muslims. Canada is home to both immigrant Muslims as well as Muslim children who were born here and raised by immigrant parents. While most Muslims live in the greater Toronto area, they also reside in other large Canadian cities such as Montreal, Vancouver, Calgary and Ottawa.

Not all Muslims are Arab or of Arab descent. In fact it is a misconception that the majority of Muslims are ethnically Arab. Muslim populations are extremely diverse in ethnic and cultural characteristics. Canadian Muslims come from Middle Eastern countries, from South Asia as well as North Africa. They can be Lebanese, Syrian, Moroccan, Algerian, Egyptian, Pakistani, Bangladeshi, Indian, Iranian or Somali. They represent various schools of religious thought or *mazhabs*, as they are called in Islamic jurisprudence. While South Asian Muslims follow the Hanafi school of jurisprudence, Arab Muslims either follow the Maliki or Shafi brand of Islam. Shia Muslims, although they too come from various ethnic backgrounds, generally follow the Jaffri school of jurisprudence. Just how retrogressive or forward-looking these juridical rulings are depends on which school of thought one adheres to.

Unveiled:

While Muslim populations burgeoned after Trudeau's immigration reforms, they have had a long presence in Canada. The first wave of Canadian Muslims came from the Balkans, prior to World War 1; the oldest mosque in Ontario is the Croatian Islamic Centre.

The Muslim population in Canada and other parts of the Western world has increased dramatically, and this has had a profound effect on the host societies. According to Mark Steyn in his book *America Alone: The End of the World as We Know It*, an increase in the populations of Muslims may even spell the demise of Western civilization's cherished institutions based on democracy, pluralism and egalitarianism. Steyn's book created an uproar in Muslim circles and sparked some human rights complaints mentioned in other chapters of this book.

Mark Steyn wrote:

> "On the Continent and everywhere else in the West, native populations are aging and fading and being supplanted remorselessly by a young Muslim demographic. Time for the obligatory "of courses". Of course not all Muslims are terrorists, though enough are hot for jihad to provide an impressive support network of mosques from Vienna to Stockholm to Toronto to Seattle. Of course not all Muslims support terrorists–though enough of them share their basic objectives (the wish to live under Islamic law in Europe and North America) to function wittingly or otherwise as the "good cop" end of an Islamic good cop/bad cop routine. But at the very minimum, this fast moving demographic transformation provides a huge comfort zone for the jihad to move around in." [1]

Of course a simple demographic shift does not automatically spell the advent of sharia in Canada. To suggest this is rather simplistic. There are indeed many Muslims who have come to Canada to escape the tyranny of sharia law. They are ardent believers in the separation of religion and state, reform within Islam and equality for Muslim women. And while many Muslims may in theory endorse orthodox belief, they do not necessarily follow every edict of the Quran, or consult it each time they plan a course of action. Only members of Muslim organizations have formulated policies affecting Muslims. It is through their work and by examining the nature of their membership that one can form an approximate view of Muslim aspirations in Canada, even though we must always accept that individuals may not follow any pattern.

Of the high profile Muslim organizations in Canada, the Muslim Canadian Congress, co-founded by author and activist Tarek Fatah, stands out as genuinely progressive. It stands for secular values and insists on the separation of religion and state in all matters of public policy. It also upholds the full equality of Muslim women. The MCC's mission statement reads: "As Muslims we believe in a progressive, liberal, pluralistic, democratic, and secular society where everyone has the freedom of religion. We want our communities to be equal and active contributors and participants in the development of a just, democratic, and equitable society in Canada." [2].

In line with its egalitarian and feminist outlook, the Muslim Canadian Congress has taken several bold but controversial positions on various issues confronting Muslim Canadians. In 2005 it organized two female-led prayers. The first prayer took place in Fatah's home and was led by author and activist Raheel Raza. The second prayer was a more public event organized at a local mosque and led by American Muslim convert Pamela Taylor. This event was significant in that it was hosted by a mosque willing to accommodate a divergent viewpoint within Islam–that women are indeed spiritual equals and competent to lead mixed-gender prayers.

The Muslim Canadian Congress, along with the Canadian Council of Muslim women, also led a forceful and effective campaign against the move to introduce sharia law in Canada. Through its many public statements, media interviews and opinion articles, the Muslim Canadian Congress impressed upon the public that sharia law, even in its most innocuous form, will systematically discriminate against Muslim women. On September 11 2005, Premiere Dalton McGuinty therefore issued a statement banning all alternative faith-based arbitration, including sharia courts.

The preservation of Canadian values based on the separation of church and state is therefore one of the primary goals of the Muslim Canadian Congress. Wherever and whenever necessary, it has also defended freedom of speech and conscience. In this regard it has often come into conflict with other Muslim organizations that have sought to restrict the right to freedom of speech, such as the moves to ban Mark Steyn's *America Alone* and block Ezra Levant's publishing of the controversial Mohammad cartoons.

The Muslim Canadian Congress has also taken a bold but controversial stance on the burka. It believes that the garment is oppressive, that it greatly marginalizes Muslim women and that it also poses a security threat.

The MCC has thus taken several courageous stands that promote the separation of religion and state and ensure women's equality under the law. In stark contrast to its position are the numerous other Muslim organizations that take a more traditional religious view of issues confronting Muslims in Canada. Notable among these are the Canadian Islamic Congress, the Islamic Supreme Council of Canada, NAMF and Cair-Can.

The Canadian Islamic Congress has openly disagreed several times with positions taken by the Muslim Canadian Congress. On one occasion, the members of the Canadian Islamic Congress even threatened to sue members of the MCC for libel. Its past president, University of Waterloo professor Mohammad Elmsary, also successfully acquired the legal rights to the MCC's name in an effort to derail its agenda. The name "Muslim Canadian Congress" is now officially owned by the Canadian Islamic Congress, all to undermine the work of the MCC, which supports gender equality and the idea of the separation of religion and state.

The CIC was also behind several human rights complaints, notably against Mark Steyn and *America Alone*. The complaints were taken to the human rights tribunals of British Columbia and Ontario. However, both tribunals dismissed the complaints. In response to the CIC's complaints to the human rights tribunals, Tarek Fatah and I wrote an article in McLean's magazine entitled *Mark Steyn has the right to be wrong*.

The CIC was also an ardent supporter of sharia tribunals in Ontario. Wahida Valiante, then vice president of the CIC, appeared in the media several times to support the right of Muslims to have their religious tribunals. Her stance was based on perceived inequality. She stated several times that if the Jewish *beit dins* were allowed to function, Muslims should also be allowed their tribunals.

The Canadian Islamic Congress has also organized the controversial Muslim history month for the last several years. The Congress believes that the media deliberately distorts Islam's image, which has contributed greatly to Islamophobia. It is therefore absolutely necessary for ordinary Canadians to be exposed to "authentic" Islamic content, in order to dispel resentment toward Muslims. Every October it organizes a national tour of speakers who "educate" Canadians about Islamic history, culture and civilization, with a focus on the contribution of Islam to the development of civilization. Islamic history month also covers the art and architecture of Islam. Mainly liberal and moderate speakers are invited to address audiences and introduce them to Islam's cultural heritage. Senator Salma Ata-Ullah Jan has also in the past addressed gatherings celebrating Islamic history month.

As benign as Islamic history month sounds, it has nonetheless managed to spark considerable controversy among some circles since its beginning in 2007. Mayor Derek Corrigan of Burnaby, British Columbia, declared the start of Islamic history month, despite several letters of protest. He responded to the protests by reaffirming Canada's policy of multiculturalism. He also cited other cultural celebrations such as "Diwali month" and "black history month" to support his stance.

The letters of protest had expressed concern that the mayor was promoting the Islamic faith to the exclusion of other faiths. However, Wahida Valiante, the vice president of the Canadian Islamic Congress, suggested that this was a way of promoting dialogue between Muslims and non-Muslims after the tragic events of 9/11.

Critics of Islamic history month, including Muslims who are members of the secular and liberal Muslim Canadian Congress, have objected to the biased picture of Islamic history that Islamic history month has so far projected. It is in line with this objection that Minister of National Defence Peter Mackay cancelled a lecture to be delivered by CIC head Imam Delic. His comments were cited by communications director Jay Paxton as follows:

"Minister MacKay took the decision to cancel the imam's role based on extremist views promulgated by the Canadian Islamic Congress (which) has declared that Israelis over the age of eighteen are legitimate targets of suicide bombers. These types of comments don't support Islamic heritage, they simply divide Canadians, promulgate hate and they have no place in Monday's celebrations. Instead, Monday's celebrations will focus on the evolution of Islam in the Canadian forces and the positive contribution of Canada's Muslim community to our society." [3]

The minister had characterized the Canadian Islamic Congress as holding extremist views. He was referring to its former president Mohammad Elmasry's earlier remarks on CTS's *Michael Coren Show* that all Israelis over eighteen are legitimate target for attacks. The Muslim Canadian Congress supported the minister's decision, stating that though Imam Delic himself was not an extremist, he had not done enough to distance himself from the positions taken by his predecessors. Nonetheless, Islamic history month takes place every year and is attended by many Muslims and non-Muslims. It also continues to spark opposition, and always for the same reasons. Writers such as Madi Lussier have continued to object on the grounds that no full month celebration of history and culture is awarded to Jews or members of other faiths. She suggests that such recognition is only to placate some Muslims who are perpetually irate over grievances. She writes:

"The newfangled "Islamic History Month" seems to ride on the coattails of the perpetually offended Muslims".[4]

The Canadian Islamic Congress is largely considered to be a Muslim advocacy group. Its positions are considered to be pro-Palestinian, pro-sharia and pro-orthodoxy. The CIC has also not taken any concrete measures to distance itself from the doctrine of armed jihad.

Unveiled:

Cair-Can is a media watchdog for perceived Islamophobic or anti-Muslim content. It keeps strict tabs on politicians, activists, and media personnel. Its role in the United States has been much more defined. However, the Canadian operation is also very vigilant about what is being said about Muslims and Islam. In order to improve its image, Cair-Can has joined hands with other Canadian Muslim organizations to denounce honour killings. After the high-profile Shafia trial, in which a father, brother and mother were convicted of killing four female family members, Cair-Can took the initiative of drafting a statement condemning the murders. However, like other more orthodox and conservative Muslim organizations, it fell short of calling the murders "honour killings". That would have immediately linked the crimes to Islam, as honour killings have now come to be associated with Islam, since most of these crimes occur in Muslim countries. Cair-Can is also actively associated with politicians. Its members, along with those of the Canadian Islamic Congress, have rallied voters to vote for candidates or parties deemed pro-Muslim. Traditionally and paradoxically, the NDP and Liberal parties of Canada have supported the more orthodox and conservative Muslim groups.

Cair-Can's website displays various position statements against hate crimes towards Muslims or Muslim groups. It keeps a very close watch on such crimes, immediately bringing them to the attention of appropriate authorities. It recently condemned an attack against a hijab-wearing woman, and also recently expressed "deep concern" about the government's CSIS information-sharing initiative.

Cair-Can was also very active in the Mahar Arrar torture case. It made a submission to the commissioner of the Arrar inquiry, detailing suggestions to introduce various policies on national security. The suggestions also included reviewing existing government policies that led to the imprisonment and subsequent torture in Syria of Canadian citizen Mahar Arrar. Cair-Can felt obligated to participate in the Arrar case as a matter of concern for a member of the Muslim community. Its president, representative Abdul-Basit Khan, stated:

"We are pleased to represent the interests of Canadian Muslims during this inquiry, and we look forward to seeing recommendations that will ensure that the rule of law and fundamental civil liberties are not sacrificed in the quest to ensure Canada's safety." [5]

Although Cair-Can has urged Muslims to build bridges with non-Muslims, its critics have grave concern about its Muslim Brotherhood roots. Lawyer David B. Harris, responding to a controversial article in the National Post by Barbara Kay, said "Barbara Kay correctly states that Cair-Can's mother organization was designated an "unindicted co-conspirator" in last year's successful *Holy Land Foundation* prosecution. [6]

It is indeed disconcerting that Cair-Can is an ultra-orthodox organization that has not produced any statements condemning the doctrine of jihad. Its main objective is upholding sharia, propagating the veiling of women, and portraying Islam and Muslims "correctly" in the media. Cair-Can also actively seeks to establish mosques in the city, and it vehemently resists any opposition to their construction. Cair-Can recently filed a lawsuit over the denial of the construction of a mosque in the greater Los Angeles area.

The Islamic Supreme Council of Canada is headed by Imam Syed Soharwardy. He is fundamentalist on several doctrinal issues but on matters of jihad and violence he has adopted the Sufi stance that Islam must be embraced by people through persuasion rather than force. He is also the founder of the organization Muslims Against Terrorism. This organization routinely condemns acts of terror committed by Muslims, but also contends that violence stems from Western domination, Israeli aggression and general interference with the culture and lifestyle of Muslims. Muslims Against Terrorism also uses theology to counter radicalism in Muslim communities. It has often cited the hadith attributed to the prophet Mohammad that a Muslim is one from whose hands and mouth all are protected. Syed Soharwardy belongs to a Sufi order, from which he derives his last name. The Sufi order believes in peaceful co-existence but nonetheless believes in the supremacy of Islam as a faith and a worldview.

The Islamic Supreme Council holds interfaith dialogues, issues statements and holds press conferences to articulate the view that Islam does not prescribe violent jihad unless it is for a just cause.

The North American Islamic Foundation, or NAMF, is a smaller organization but actively pursues an Islamist agenda. NAMF runs schools, charitable organizations and prayer services–all geared toward inculcating an Islamic mindset rooted in tradition. Its female students come to school fully covered, and learn about Islam's history of conquest and domination in their school environment.

Herein lies the problem with most Islamic outfits in Canada and across the rest of the world. Author, activist and founder of the Muslim Canadian Congress, Tarek Fatah, rightly says that it is only by Muslim organizations across Canada and the world clearly repudiating the doctrine of armed jihad that this fight can be won. That repudiation is a long time coming. Jihad, being an important tenet of Islam, poses a theological challenge. Unless this challenge is met at the theological level, it is a tall order to expect Muslims to distance themselves from it.

Unveiled:

Soharwardy has tried to provide a theological challenge to it by promoting the Sufi brand of Islam. Other sects of Islam, such as the Ahmedia, also believe in jihad as a personal struggle. The Ahmedia, however, have been castigated by the majority of Muslims as non-Muslim.

Contrary to the popular tide of Wahhabi fundamentalism that focuses on monotheism rather than on the personality of the prophet, Soharwardy's supreme council holds celebrations for the prophet Mohammad's birthday, and holds gatherings in praise of the prophet periodically. Soharwardy has hence lost favour with more radical groups whose main focus is to proliferate Islam, through violence if necessary. But like other Muslim organizations, The Islamic Supreme Council of Canada also actively works hard to defend orthodoxy and to protect the civil liberties of Muslims, along with their religious rights, their culture and their very presence in North America.

The above is merely a glimpse of what some major Muslim organizations and their memberships hold dear. If their membership indicates the pulse of a segment of the Muslim community in Canada, then the majority of Muslims who engage in activism belong to the more traditional schools of thought within Islam. However, most Muslims living in Canada do not in fact attend mosques, although attendees have increased steadily. The majority of Canadian Muslims also do not seek membership in Muslim organizations.

Most Canadian Muslim organizations remain orthodox. With the exception of the Muslim Canadian Congress, no Muslim organization has genuinely repudiated the doctrine of armed jihad or fought for women's equality. That is the need of the hour and one that all Muslim organizations must embrace.

How Islamists are Changing Canada

As a liberal and reform-minded Muslim, I am deeply concerned over the dents in Canada's liberal democracy. I believe it risks being greatly compromised by Islamist influences, due to an influx of Muslim immigrants from conservative Muslim backgrounds. They believe in upholding sharia, they work to insulate their children from foreign or Western influences, they exert pressure on their daughters to marry before they complete high school, they engage in surreptitious polygamous unions and they work tirelessly to demand outrageous faith accommodations in Canada's public schools. These Islamists also work toward propagating the burka, niqab and hijab among Muslim women with a ferocity that renders these women helpless in the face of such religious oppression. Canada's landscape is changing rapidly as a result. Fifteen years ago almost no niqabi women were to be seen on the streets of Toronto. We naturally prize a diverse and free society where all citizens enjoy the right to freedom of religion, but we must look deeper to unearth the oppression that gives only the illusion of freedom of choice for young Muslim women. Many of these women, especially from countries like Somalia, are even being subjected to brutally misogynistic practices such as female genital mutilation.

Islamist men who believe in polygamy are engaging in it right here in Canada. Imam Ally Hindi of Toronto has publicly admitted to performing these polygamous marriages, sometimes advising these cheating husbands to keep mum about their secret unions, and especially not to divulge these to their first wives. Hindi's mosque is being funded by Saudi Arabia. Here is a culture of deception being promoted by a well-known imam. Canada's policy of multiculturalism unfortunately enables such subcultures to thrive within its borders, despite the systematic gender-based discrimination they preach. The influx of Muslims with such beliefs is not only changing the society of Canada; it is also reshaping its public institutions in disquieting ways.

I very strongly believe that public schools in Canada should be insulated from any type of religious indoctrination. I have experienced it first hand at a number of schools in the GTA. When my children were finally admitted to the neighbourhood public school in 1995, they reported some disturbing incidents that occurred in the school playground. These were comments by other Muslim children that were derogatory to non-Muslim children. One Muslim child went around telling other kids that they were all doomed to eternal hellfire. He must have heard this belief expressed at home. Since I was a member of the parent council, this incident was brought to my attention by a distraught mother. She stated to me plainly that while she respected the beliefs of others, she did not appreciate the bigotry which this child expressed towards non-Muslim children. She also complained to me about the grade three Muslim teacher who had refused to shake hands with her and other mothers. They had felt insulted, and rightly so. Every single interaction between men and women is seen as lascivious. Must even shaking hands hold sexual innuendo?

Such taboos, paranoia and prejudice are common among fundamentalist Muslims. Family friends of ours who have turned fanatically religious espouse this sort of line. Before the lady of the house suddenly discovered deep piety, she had socialized with male friends. One of them paid the family a surprise visit after her new found religiosity. Since the husband was away, she refused to let this long-time male friend in for fear of sexual tension or simply the suspicion his presence might have raised in others. Those are the types of strictures that some conservative Muslim families observe even in Canada.

To live strictly according to sharia is the goal of conservative Muslim families in Canada. These are values they are imparting to their young children as well. They live in constant fear of violating some of these tenets. I have often argued that sharia is all man-made and Muslims need not feel bound by it. Sharia simply comprises interpretations of the canonical texts of Islam.

For this reason, the public school system in Ontario has seen a surge in demands by Muslims to make all sorts of faith accommodations. Permanent prayer rooms are being established everywhere. Muslim children are being exposed to the tenets of this man-made sharia code from the very start. Little wonder they show contempt for non-Muslim children. The cafeteria in Valley Park Middle School in Toronto is turned into a prayer hall for Friday prayers, catering to a good four hundred Muslim students. The school authorities and the Toronto District School Board believe that this is less disruptive for the students, as they would otherwise simply leave for Friday prayers and never return. That is odd; surely the school should simply adopt firm disciplinary measures to ensure students return to class, rather than turn public property into a mosque. The school cafeteria has now come to be known as Mosqueteria, and with good reason. Liberal MPP Kathleen Wynne favours this type of faith accommodation. "We've had religious accommodation in our schools for many years. We are simply providing space. It's a practice that's making us stronger," [1] she said.

At a rally in 2011 organized by the Canadian Secular Alliance, I made the argument that the school must not endorse discrimination against female students, who are always made to sit in the back of a prayer session. The Toronto District School Board, however, seems to have turned a blind eye to the genuine concerns people have raised about such gender-based discrimination in school.

It is not just in prayer that Muslim girls face discrimination. They are barred from attending swimming classes or even at times gym classes unless they can wear long clothes that cover every inch of their tiny bodies. Many Muslim girls, even as young as eight and nine, are forced to wear the hijab in school. Muslim children are also sometimes barred from attending music class and sex education class. I am aware of this because as a faith leader I have been invited to examine the faith accommodations sought by various faith communities by the Peel District School Board in Mississauga. These meetings have been attended by very conservative imams who make their agenda known unequivocally. They have clearly objected to sex education and any music and cultural activity involving co-ed participation.

These are some ways in which the conservative Muslim community wishes to influence public education. Such accommodations would be acceptable if they did not diminish opportunities for Muslim children, especially girls. Unfortunately they do, and Muslim girls, who already do not have much of a voice, are the ones who suffer the negative consequences of such accommodations. Proponents of multiculturalism do not see the effects of such accommodations on women and girls. They see only the Muslim community as a whole, and readily submit to demands that are often quite outrageous because they discriminate systematically against females.

The education authorities also want to bend over backward to accommodate such demands. Recently, the provincial Minister of Education Lauren Broten agreed to establish Muslim prayer halls at London and Kitchener secondary Catholic schools, in response to demands by Muslim students. These are obviously schools which stress Catholic values, yet they tolerate various faiths and beliefs that are quite different from Catholicism. Perhaps Muslims can learn a thing or two about religious tolerance through this example. Muslims tend to be more devout than other faith communities and happen to be the only religious group demanding such accommodations. Unilateral Muslim demands are producing an exclusive Muslim religious presence in schools that are supposed to showcase the diversity that is Canada.

Canada's liberal democracy is also greatly compromised in other ways. While conservative Muslims want others to tolerate their religious beliefs, they refuse to afford such tolerance to others. The minute there is some opposition to Islamic belief, or some negative portrayal in the media of Muslim practice, conservative Muslims begin to level accusations of racism, Islamophobia or Western conspiracy. Unfortunately Muslims believe it is their exclusive right to be accommodated because they are the bearers of the One True God's final message. This underlying attitude needs to be addressed if the Muslim psyche is to emerge from the dark ages. Elitism and religious arrogance serve no community well in the connected world of the twenty-first century.

In my opinion, the most significant change in the West due to Islamism and an influx of fundamentalist Muslims is a restriction of freedom of speech. Westerners are now scared to criticize Islam or Muslim practice openly. They have witnessed Muslim rage across the world over perceived insults to Islam and step lightly in order not to anger Muslims. If they criticize Islam or Muslims, they couch it in language that is evasive and euphemistic. In this regard, I have recently seen tweets by Westerners who think the anti-Islam Mohammad movie should not be aired for fear of inciting Muslim anger. Recently a documentary entitled *Islam: the Untold Story* by historian Tom Holland was banned from being shown a second time on the BBC because several Muslims and Muslim organizations wrote angry and threatening emails.

There have been many such attempts to limit citizens' democratic rights to freedom of speech. The Canadian Islamic Congress has often attempted to put such limits on Canadians. The most famous case was of course the complaint to the Human Rights Tribunal about Mark Steyn's book, *America Alone*. There has also been a push to transform Canada by demanding institutional change such as sharia law. Parallel cultures that promote inequality within the dominant tradition of Canada's egalitarian laws can never be acceptable. Yet such minority courts had been functioning in Ontario before Dalton McGuinty banned them in 2005.

Some issues have also become highly politicized in Canadian educational institutions. The Israeli/Palestinian conflict, for example, features each year at the University of Toronto's Israel apartheid week. Tensions are usually high. Inflamed rhetoric leads to further tensions among ethnic and religious groups.

Any further influx of immigrants espousing such radical views can be expected to heighten such conflicts even further.

It is enlightening to look at *Statistics Canada, Projections of the Diversity of the Canadian Population: 2006 to 2031*. According to this report, immigrants, defined simply as people born in foreign lands, will form an ever-larger percentage of the Canadian population. The report estimates the number of foreign-born to be around 14.5 million by 2031, compared to just 3.8 million in 1981. Immigrants would therefore constitute roughly thirty-two percent of the Canadian population in the year 2031. Among immigrants, Muslims are estimated to be the fastest-growing community, as they attract some converts and Muslims tend to have larger families. According to the same projections, the Muslim population will triple between now and 2031, by which year it will comprise 7.3 percent of the total population.

Of course, numbers alone do not usher in a caliphate, a sharia-based economy or a complete transformation of schools into madrassahs. But the old adage that there is strength in numbers will certainly enable the radical forces to continue demanding even more faith accommodations than the ones we have already seen. Certainly, the Muslims who are in Canada because they wish to escape the tyranny of sharia law would not demand this. However, the vociferous and doctrinaire Islamists will most certainly pressure Canada's public institutions to accommodate their retrogressive agenda.

Perhaps the most promising way to deter such an outcome is to empower modernist Muslim voices within Canada. I firmly believe that there are many Muslims who are sick and tired of backwardness in their community, who find the agenda of the Islamists ultimately damaging to them and their children. But they are just too afraid to speak out for fear of the Islamists, who attempt to silence every voice of dissent. They are the bullies in schools, mosques and even homes.

Hopefully this book will in some small way help to open the door to discourse on Islam's intersection with the West. Liberal, secular and progressive Muslims must shed their fears and join the present lone voices of dissent against the obscurantist forces in our midst. They must begin by understanding that there is no systematic racism in Canada. Any conflict between Islam and the West is not a debate about ethnicities or cultural backgrounds or racial prejudice. It is a debate over values and sensibilities which can be regarded as universal. Do we tolerate misogyny? Do we tolerate restrictions on freedom of speech? Do we believe in liberal democracy? Do we allow our daughters to make their own major decisions about their lives, including the man they wish to marry? Do we let them choose what to wear? Do we let them receive an enlightening

Unveiled:

education and allow them to follow their dreams, even if those dreams involve music, or theatre or art? We need liberal Muslims to step up to the challenge and grasp an opportunity here to defeat the Islamists in their proliferation of an oppressive ideology. This takes a lot of courage. I have spoken openly in this book to help set a precedent in the pursuit of equality, civility and humanity.

Modernizing Islam

My desire to contribute to the modernization of Islam emerged from my commitment to the precepts my faith and my determination to see it adapt and improve. While I firmly believe in secular governance and the separation of religion and state, I know that people from the Middle East, South Asia and Africa are still strongly influenced by religious law and circumscribed by religious taboos. Religion continues to play a vital role in the lives of Muslims, which is why I consider the issue of modernizing or moderating Islam both crucial and sensitive. It is one that touches on vital concerns, such as how a society might deliver basic human rights to its marginalized people. The world has progressed far beyond seventh century Arabia, when Islamic injunctions were introduced to a Bedouin society. The modern world has come to recognize the dignity of all people, regardless of gender, race, creed and colour. This inclusive recognition has been enshrined in the United Nations Declaration of Human Rights. The dignity of every member of the human family has been acknowledged in the following sentence: "Whereas the peoples of the United Nations have in the Charter reaffirmed their faith in fundamental human rights, in the dignity and worth of the human person and in the equal rights of men and women and have determined to promote social progress and better standards of life in larger freedom."[1]

Many Islamic nations did not sign the UDHR, perhaps suggesting that their women and religious minorities are not considered fully human under sharia law. Indeed, in 1982 an Iranian UN official declared that the UDHR contravened Islamic values. Forty-eight countries ratified the UDHR, while six Communist countries abstained, as well as Saudi Arabia, the cradle of Islam.

Unveiled:

Especially after the 9/11 attacks, I have come across several attempts to reinterpret Islam, most of which tried to reconcile Islam with modern inclusive ideas. Understandings of Islam range from the most retrogressive to the secular and liberal. The latter includes scholars like Abdullahi An-Naim and writers like Tarek Fatah, who have tried to argue for political reform within Islam. They have postulated the view that Islam is merely a system of beliefs and rituals and should not aspire to be a political movement. In other words, there is no need to establish a state based on Islamic principles. As long as a Muslim majority state remains neutral religiously, Islam can be practiced freely without hindrances.

I set out to examine some of these opinions in order to understand what Islam really stood for. First, I was interested in determining whether Islam is merely a system of beliefs or if it is also a political force.

Most Muslims, whether actively religious or not, believe that Islam will eventually prevail over all other worldviews. For this to materialize, a form of governance with legislation rooted in divine edicts must be put in place. This view was formalized in the medieval Muslim philosopher Al-Mavardi's writings. He emphasized the need for such a state because the faith must be safeguarded at all costs. I had read Al-Mawardi's writings as a young woman. Needless to say, modern Islamists, be they militants or "soft" Islamists, draw inspiration from such religious aspirations. They find further support for their opinion in historical precedent, stressing that the prophet was not only a religious leader but also a statesman who ruled the nascent Islamic city-state of Medina. As he was the divine spokesman of the Quran, the prophet's example must be followed and therefore Muslims of all subsequent generations must establish a state that replicates the first "Islamic state". Also at the core of this viewpoint is the belief that sovereignty belongs to God alone, therefore God's rule and God's laws must be established on earth.

My friend Tarek Fatah, founder of the Muslim Canadian Congress, questioned this view in his book *Chasing a Mirage: The Tragic Illusion of an Islamic State*. He substantiated his claims through an analysis of both historical and contemporary Islamic societies. He argued that the absence of explicit injunctions in the Quran for Muslims to establish such a state absolves them of any obligation to revive a global caliphate or to create a theocratic state. He confirmed that the prophet Mohammed did not name a successor or devise a comprehensive system of Islamic governance.

Though Fatah's conclusions may be reasonable from a modernist perspective, his stance would not be accepted universally or readily among Muslims, some of whom accept rival theological interpretations. These theological arguments in fact comprise some of the roadblocks toward reform. For example, many might insist that even though Islam does not specify a form of government, establishing an Islamic state is still imperative based on the arguments that Al-Mavardi proposed. It is up to Islamic communities to develop mechanisms for good governance, but the state must still be based on sharia law as an acknowledgment of God's sovereignty on earth.

Emory University Professor Abdullahi An-Naim published a book the same year called *Islam and the Secular State: Negotiating the Future of Sharia*. He came to Toronto to discuss his ideas, where I met him briefly after the lecture. He claimed that because Muslim beliefs are so diverse, there should be no state religion. This he regarded as an Islamic reason for the idea of separation of religion and state. In effect, An-Naim merely suggests an Islamic version of the Jeffersonian model of a "wall between religion and state."

I find Fatah's position, like that of An-Naim, rational and desirable, because it demands that an archaic political worldview be abandoned. Naim cites history to support the thesis that an Islamic state never did exist, nor was it ever a religious requirement. But in the quest for reform, rationality is often compromised when orthodox Muslims cling to immutable worldviews.

The most troubling aspects of Islamic sharia pertain to women. Traditional Muslims accept its inequality. They believe that the apparent disparity in gender rights is not really a disparity and must be viewed holistically. Any inequalities are there for a good reason and they ultimately must benefit society as a whole. Obviously such Muslims would not insist on "reforming Islam" through a reinterpretation. Most Muslim activists and scholars probably hold this view. They are happy with the provisions of the Quran about women and do not feel the need to change anything. According to them, Islam is perfect as it is, and anything perfect by definition does not require change or modification. When change is not necessary, it is necessary not to change.

I have come across many fundamentalist Muslims who reject outright any notions of modernizing Islam. In their opinion Islam is regarded as a comprehensive philosophy that has answers for all of mankind's problems. Even suggesting that Islam is in need of reform is sacrilege to them. These people regard Islam's provisions, even the ones that seem blatantly unjust to a non-Muslim, as having a purpose aimed at an inscrutable higher good, such as the good of society as a whole.

Another category of Muslims believes that there is indeed a need to reconcile not Islam itself, but a retrogressive understanding of Islam, with modernity. This group of reformers also believes Islam to be a perfect set of beliefs and practices, but also asserts that it has come to be misapplied, misinterpreted and therefore misrepresented through the centuries. They believe that

Unveiled:

Quranic verses need to be revisited, that they lend themselves to various interpretations that our contemporary enlightened values will very readily accept.
They therefore argue for reinterpreting Quranic verses in order to render them
more female-friendly. For example, they contend that men and women are indeed equal in the Quran, not just in a spiritual sense, but also with respect to
social regulations. They insist that a different approach to the Quran will allow
us to recognize this. They believe that the inequality has evolved because the
words of the Quran have been mistranslated.

Other groups of reformers believe that around the advent of Islam, social conditions were deplorable in many respects and Islam represented a moral advancement for the time, but that modern societies have progressed beyond
those parochial conditions and have forged a new world that transcends differences of race, creed, colour or gender. According to this group of reformers,
Islam falls short of modern notions of gender equality or racial harmony, and
its tenets clash with modern democratic movements and their notions of lib-
eralism, freedom of conscience and gender equality.

I therefore perceive three distinct discourses within Islam on women's rights.
The first is the one vigorously promoted by Dr. Farhat Hashmi, which attempts
to render women invisible and anonymous by enshrouding them in burkas, endorsing polygamous marriages and upholding the uncontested guardianship
of the husband over the wife. Ironically such a discourse claims to be progressive, based on the "complementarity" argument, this time applied to the letter.
The second, a slightly more progressive discourse, does not entirely strive to
subjugate women by confining them in gender specific roles, but nonetheless
emphasizes the need to reclaim the "rights" Muslim women enjoyed under
Islam many centuries ago. This is dangerous, in my opinion, because it will
not lead toward progress, but rather toward seventh-century norms which are
hopelessly inappropriate in modern society. This is by far the most prevalent
discourse among Muslim women who are self-proclaimed "feminists" out to
reclaim their rights. Yet it is no longer enough simply to reclaim these rights.
While this will improve conditions for a segment of Muslim women in some
societies, it will fall hopelessly short of modern standards of gender equality
under the law. The third strain of course demands full equality for Muslim
women—a view I endorse wholeheartedly. But even with respect to women's
equality, reformers have struck theological hurdles. Laleh Bakhtiar is an Ira-
nian-American scholar and activist who recently translated the Quran from a
feminist perspective. I met Laleh at a women's conference, and she agreed to
send me her book.

In her commentary she argued that the contentious verse 4: 34 of the Quran,
which appoints men as the guardians of women and therefore grants them

the right to chastise them or even beat them, does not really suggest a physical beating. She suggests the terminology of the Quran actually means that rebellious women should be left alone and that men must "walk away from them." Other scholars, such as Riffat Hassan, have argued that the problem is not with the religious texts of Islam per se, but with their interpretation. Hassan has said that the Arabic language, rich in meanings as it is, not only can lend itself to modernist readings, but that its modernist readings would in fact be the more authentic renditions of the text. Her interpretation implies that Adam for example was not a man, but simply a being (possibly female) created out of the dust of the earth. The etymology of the word Adam, she insists, lends itself to this type of female-friendly reading. However, such readings are often rejected by orthodox Muslims.

Thus many reformers have focused their attention on modernizing the readings of the Islamic canonical texts. These scholars have included Ahmed Ali, Mohammad Asad, Laleh Bakhtair, Riffat Hassan, Amina Wadud and Khaled abul Fadl, to mention a few.

According to our modern perceptions, the parts of the Quran which need revisiting include those that touch on polygamy, unequal inheritance shares for women, punishments for adultery, the fact that a woman's testimony is considered half of a man's, the fact that husbands can pronounce a divorce so readily, and the fact that the custody of children is invariably granted to the father.

The plight of religious minorities in Muslim countries is another troubling issue. Why do minorities have to pay extra tax for their lives and livelihoods to remain protected? To any contemporary person, Muslim or non-Muslim, this is blatant injustice. According to authentic Islamic sources, the jizya tax is justified because non-Muslims are not required to undertake jihad. In order for the Muslim state to provide them protection, it must impose a tax in lieu of the zakat which Muslims pay. Jihad is a religious duty for Muslims; so be it. But Christians should not be exploited financially simply because jihad is not part of their religious tradition. Religious minorities living in an Islamic state are indeed vulnerable to the point that if they do not pay the jizya, they might even lose their lives. All of these provisions offend our modern sensibilities. They have in fact prompted reform-minded Muslims like myself to seek solutions by formulating a modern approach religion. This would entail a clear repudiation of all of these prescriptions.

Can our modern sensibilities permit a state configured on sharia provisions like the above? And what about the notion of jihad itself? Don't modern provisions of international law forbid religious warfare, and therefore shouldn't jihad be shunned as a doctrine of the past? The question then is how to reconcile

141

these provisions with modern sensibilities. Is there another approach to Islam and the Quran that can enable this agreement?

Islam is what it is. But can it be moderated? I believe it can. I also believe the solutions lie within Islam's own philosophical framework. For example, the concept of *ijithad* needs to be modernized itself. It has traditionally been defined as free or independent thinking to arrive at a juristic ruling on issues over which the Quran and *hadith* are silent. The efforts of the eighth and ninth century jurists such as Imam Shaffi and Abu Hanifah came about as a result of such *ijtihad*, as these doctors of jurisprudence were exercising independent reasoning to interpret legal sources by responding to the changing conditions of society. *Ijtihad* needs to evolve from its earlier manifestations by being freely altered to suit modern conditions.

Less commonly known is the fact that an earlier group of exegetes of the Quran, known as the *Ahl-Ra'aay*, considered rationality and the principle of *istihsaan* (juristic preference to arrive at the most equitable solution) a paramount principle in deducing religious law. They strove for a just society that would accommodate the rights of all, while paying special attention to the rights of the weak and underprivileged. Unfortunately, over time the principle of *istihsaan* came to be sidelined and the doctrine of *taqlid* or blind following of traditional schools of jurisprudence gained ascendancy.

Any progressive approach to religion must revive the concept of *istihsaan* as a first step toward delivering justice and equality to all in a Muslim society. It must also reconsider the Quran's time-specific social laws, its broad normative principles and its overall objective of creating a just society that would treat members with equality and fairness.

The Quran has time-specific injunctions and normative principles. Regrettably, the Quran's overarching principles of justice and fairness have been ignored because too much attention has been paid to the temporal legal injunctions of the Quran. The application of sharia law in Pakistan produces unequal inheritance rights for women, and unjust dispensations of cases involving alimony, child custody, divorce, and polygamy. This is because it is obsessed with conforming to specific seventh century expressions of Quranic principles, which has led to the repression and marginalization of Muslim women and minorities.

I like to emphasize the Quran's broad principles instead of its specifics. One must look at the principles behind Quranic edicts rather than their specific applications in seventh century Arabia. The Quran's principles of fairness, compassion, justice and equity need to be expressed as full equality for women in the contemporary context, where notions of gender equality, peace, tolerance and harmony have been refined to a point where such rights are considered inalienable. The Quran, through planting the seeds for such reform within the context of its own revelation, showed the path for future reform and progress towards universally recognized human values.

Even within the Quran there was no stagnation. The Quran too had abrogated some of its earlier prescriptions and replaced them with ones that were more suited to the changing conditions. I therefore believe that accommodating change is in itself a Quranic principle. I do not propose that Muslims should abandon Quranic principles. They can merely express the same principles in ways that are more equitable. Polygamy may have seemed like an equitable solution in the seventh century when women had no other recourse. However now it is no longer so when women can easily fend for themselves.

I believe that moderating or modernizing Islam is not impossible. Bringing it in harmony with modern sensibilities is a task I have personally undertaken through my writings. In my book *Islam, Women and the Challenges of Today* I pointed out that Islamic injunctions in seventh century Arabia had represented a moral advancement in the rights of women, of the downtrodden and of racially marginalized groups. Islam brought about a social and cultural revolution at the time. The Quran itself provided many injunctions that benefited various groups. But were the Quranic injunctions supposed to be interpreted literally, for all times? In improving the lot of women and slaves, did the Quran provide a principle for continued progress for all times? The same principle of progress could be applied to achieve even greater equality for women and marginalized groups as societies evolve.

In the end, I urge all Muslims, fundamentalist and liberal, to think long and hard about these issues. It is now time to shun bigotry and obscurantism to enable a better future for all. I also urge Muslims to embrace Canadian values of equality, pluralism and dignity for all human beings. They must discard their anti-Western sentiment. They have chosen Canada as their home and they owe allegiance to it.

Glossary

abaya	loose garment, usually black, worn by Muslim women over regular clothes
beit din	Jewish Rabbinical court
biddat/biddah	later addition to orthodox belief
burka	full-length cloak worn over normal attire, covering the entire body and face
chador	loose garment that drapes the body
daf	seventh century drum-like musical instrument
dhimmi	non-believer who has a protected status in an Islamic state
diyat	blood money sometimes offered in lieu of punishment for murder
duppata	long garment used to cover the hair
Eid	Islamic festival
fatwa	religious opinion
ghazwaat	war fought by the early Muslims
gunah kabira	a grave sin
hadith	oral tradition attributed to Mohammad
hadood of God	laws in Ziaul Haqq's Pakistan, based on so-called limits
Hajj	annual pilgrimage to Mecca
haqq-tafweez	delegated right of divorce given to the wife by her husband
haram	prohibited
hijab	Islamic headscarf
iftar	meal eaten at the breaking of the fast in Ramadan
ijithad	independent or personal judgment in legal matters
istihsaan	juristic preference seeking the most just solution

jihad	religious warfare
jizya	tax levied on non Muslims in an Islamic state
Kaaba	shrine at the centre of the grand mosque in Mecca
kafir	person who rejects faith
kalmia	Muslim profession of faith
mazhab	school of jurisprudence
nasheed	songs of praise for the prophet Mohammad
nikah	Muslim marriage ceremony
niqab	veil covering the face
saee	symbolic run between hills during pilgrimage to commemorate Hagar's struggle
salat	ritual Islamic prayer
sedar	Jewish feast marking Passover
shalwar kameez	two-piece South Asian dress
sharia	comprehensive moral and religious code of Islam
sooq	Arabic market
tablighi	Muslim evangelist
tajweed	rhythmic recitation of the Quran
taqlid	blind following of orthodox opinions
taqwa	piety
Umrah	smaller pilgrimage to Mecca
Wahhabi	puritanical and severe movement within Islam
zakat	fourth pillar of Islam enjoining charity

Notes

Chapter 1: Terror over Blue Skies

1. Andrea Elliott, "For Times Sq. Suspect, Long Roots of Discontent," *New York Times*, www.NYTimes.com (accessed May 16, 2012).

2. Iftekhar, Hai, "Renewal of Islamic Values," www.umaia.net (accessed February 12, 2012).

3. Andrea Elliott, "For Times Sq. Suspect, Long Roots of Discontent," *New York Times*, www.NYTimes.com (accessed May 16, 2012).

Chapter 5: Honour Killings: Causes and Solutions

1. Canadian Council of Muslim Women, "CCMW Position on Customary Killings," www.ccmw.com (accessed July 6, 2012).

2. Phyllis Chesler, "Worldwide Trends in Honor Killings," *The Middle East Quarterly*, Spring 2010, 3-11.

Chapter 6: The Sharia Debate

1. Joanne Bailey,"Islam Doesn't Oppress Me," The Union of Islamic World Students, www.Rohama.org (accessed March 11, 2012).

Chapter 7: The Burka Debate

1. Nikki.R. Keddie, *Women in the Middle East: Past and Present* (Princeton University Press, 2007), 13.

2. Nikki.R Keddie, *Women in the Middle East: Past and Present* (Princeton University Press, 2007), 14.

3. Katherine Bullock, *Rethinking Muslim Women and the Veil* (The International Instituteof Islamic Thought, 2003), 183.

4. Katherine Bullock, *Rethinking Muslim Women and the Veil* (The International Institute of Islamic Thought, 2003), 215.

Chapter 8: A Decade Opposing Jihadism

1. Mohammad Marmaduke Pickthall, *The Glorious Quran* (Lahore, Taj Company, 1977), 65.

2. Mohammad Asad, *The Message of the Quran* (Lahore, Dar al-Andalus Limited, 1980), 41.

3. Mohammad Marmaduke Pickthall, *The Glorious Quran* (Lahore, Taj Company, 1977), 68.

4. John L. Esposito, *The Islamic Threat: Myth or Reality* (Oxford, Oxford University Press, 1999), 10.

5. John L. Esposito, *The Islamic Threat: Myth or Reality* (Oxford, Oxford University Press, 1999), 11.

6. Syed Ameer Ali, *The Spirit of Islam* (New Delhi, Kitab Bhawan, 1977), 56.

Chapter 12: Islam and Music: a Conflict Within

1. Abu Bilal Mustafa Al-Kanadi, "Music and Singing in the Light of the Quran and Sunnah," www.islamworld.net (accessed June, 16 2012).

Chapter 14: Muslims in Canada

1. Mark Steyn, America Alone: *The End of the World As We Know It* (Washington: Regnery Publishing Inc, 2006), 33.

2. Muslim Canadian Congress, "The MCC Mission," www.muslimcanadiancongress.org (accessed June 7, 2012).

3. Madi Lussier, "Gift of fear" CIReport (2011), www.cireport.ca (accessed July 10, 2012).

4. Abdul Basit Khan's statements, www.cair-can.ca (accessed July 7, 2012).

5. David B. Harris, "Harris Condemns Islamist Cair-Can and its Apologist, the taxpayer-funded Centre for Faith and the Media," Point de Bascule www.pointdebascule.ca

Chapter 15: How Islamists are Changing Canada

1. Christina Blizzard, "For Heaven's Sake" *Toronto Sun*, www.torontosun.com (accessed September 11, 2012).

Chapter 16: Modernizing Islam

1. Preamble: The Universal Declaration of Human Rights, http://www.un.org/en/documents/udhr/index.shtml (accessed September 18, 2012).

Bibliography

Afsaruddin, Asma. 2008. *The First Muslims: History and Memory.* Oxford: One World.

Ali, Parveen Shaukat. 1997. *Politics of Conviction: The Life and Times of Muhammad Zia-ul-*

Haq. London: The London Centre for Pakistan Studies.

Ali, Syed Ameer. *The Spirit of Islam: A History of the Evolution and Ideals of Islam,*

with a Life of the Prophet. New Delhi: Kitab Bhavan.

Anisuddin, Syed. 2011. *Democracy and Islam.* New Delhi: Adam Publishers and Distributors.

An-Naim, Abdullahi Ahmed. 2008. *Islam and the Secular State: Negotiating the Future of*

Sharia. Cambridge: Harvard University Press.

Armstrong, Karen. 2008. *Islam: A Short History revised ed.* New York: Modern Library.

Barlas, Asma. 2002. *Believing Women in Islam: Unreading Patriarchal Interpretations of the*

Quran. Karachi: Sama Editorial and Publishing Services.

Bullock, Katherine. 2003. *Rethinking Muslim Women and the Veil.* London: The International Institute of Islamic Thought.

Bakhtiar, Laleh. 2009. *The Sublime Quran.* Chicago: Kazi Publications.

Daniel, Norman. 2000. *Islam and the West: The Making of an Image reprint ed.* Oxford: One World.

Esposito, John L. 1998. *Islam: The Straight Path 3rd ed.* New York: Oxford University Press.

Fatah, Tarek. *Chasing a Mirage: The Tragic Illusion of an Islamic State.* Toronto: John,

Wiley & Sons 2008.

Haq, Mazhural. 1977. *A Short History of Islam.* Lahore: Ripon Printing Press.

Keddie, Nikki R. 2007. *Women in the Middle East: Past and Present.* Princeton: Princeton University Press.

Nomani, Asra. 2005. *Standing Alone in Mecca.* SanFrancisco: Harper.

Phares, Walid. 2010. *The Coming Revolution: Struggle for Freedom in the Middle East*. New York: Threshold Editions.

Peters, Rudolph. 1996. *Jihad in Classical and Modern Islam: A Reader*. Princeton: NJ: Markus Wiener.

Yusuf al Qaradawi. 2006. *The Lawful and the Prohibited in Islam*. New Delhi: Kitab Bhawan

Renard, John. 1998. *101 Questions and Answers on Islam*. New York: Gramercy Books.

Rashid, Ahmed. 2000. *Taliban: Militant Islam, Oil and Fundamentalism in Central Asia*. New Haven, London: Yale University Press.

Serajuddin, Alamgir Muhammad. 2001. *Shari'a Law and Society: Tradition and Change in South Asia*. Oxford: Oxford University Press.

Wadud, Amina. 1999. *Quran and Women: Rereading the Sacred Texts from a Woman's Perspective*. New York, Oxford: Oxford University Press.

CPSIA information can be obtained at www.ICGtesting.com
Printed in the USA
LVOW041234281112

309072LV00005B/36/P

9 780988 169159